The Hollies

A HOME FOR CHILDREN

Children walking with a Housemother, 1949.

The Hollies

A HOME FOR CHILDREN

Jad Adams & Gerry Coll

LONDON 2005

First published in 2005
by the Authors

© 2005 Jad Adams and Gerry Coll
Copyright of individual accounts is held by their contributors

The right of Jad Adams and Gerry Coll
to be identified as the authors of this work
has been asserted by them in accordance with
the Copyright, Design and Patents Act 1988

A catalogue record for this book
is available from the British Library

ISBN 0-9548993-0-X
Cover and book design
Vera Brice and Leslie Robinson

Printed and bound in Great Britain
by St Edmundsbury Press
Blenheim Industrial Park, Newmarket Road
Bury St Edmunds, Suffolk IP33 3TZ

This book is dedicated to
all those children
who have experienced the care system.

Acknowledgements

Many thanks and gratitude to the people who felt able to sponsor this book.

I am grateful to all my many friends and associates, whose support helped me. I am happy to say there are more of them than I can acknowledge by name here. But you know who you are and I thank you eternally.

Many thanks to Mrs Katherine Harding and Mrs Denise Baldwin for their permission to reproduce part of The Early Beginnings: A Brief History of the Area featured in the *Burnt Oak School Centenary 1903-2003*, printed by Bexley Council Graphics 600018/7.03. Thanks are due to Mr John Mercer for his permission to use 'The Hollies' manuscript. Thanks to Southwark NALGO for permission to quote from 'The Hollies Case for an Independent Inquiry'.

Many thanks to Babs for her brilliant Website:
http://groups.msn.com/childrenhomesuk.commonwealth/home.htm

Staff at the London Metropolitan Archives gave valuable assistance and permission to use photographs. Special thanks to Julian Watson, Frances Ward, Jenny O'Keefe and Wendy Walker, Staff at the Greenwich Heritage Centre, for illustrations used with their kind permission. To Simon McKeon, Centre Manager, Local Studies Centre, Bexley, and to Oliver Wooller, Frances Sweeny and Linda McCann for their assistance, co-operation and permission to reproduce black and white photographs. To Gillian Richies for illustrations accompanying Rose Lloyds' account. To Ray and Sue Wheeler for their continued encouragement. Grateful acknowledgement to Bexley Council and Brenda Johnson as artist for reproduction of her illustration of buildings as they appear today. Remembering Ann and Chris Wyse. Special thanks to Megan O'Brien and Yasmin Lodrick-Osborn for their assistance in typing the text copy; and to Vera Brice for the typesetting. You did splendid work. To St Edmundsbury Press, especially to Denis Harman, for his professional guidance.

To Vera and Leslie, who never cease to impress me as a design team, with their unparalleled knowledge of book design and publishing; forever indebted to you both.

vii

The Sponsors

Michael McCarthy

Des and Rowena O'Brien

Our Lady of the Rosary RC Church, Blackfen

Michael and Charlotte Rice

Alan and Rita Passey

Raymond and Sara Dunning

Gerry and Mary Oliver

Eileen and Tony Fleming

Mr and Mrs John Murphy

Heather Holden

Paul Smith

Gabrielle and Brendan Joyce

Margaret Chater

David Rice

Dr Griffin

Mick and Jean Cunvin

Paul Beven

Newton and Mary Abrew

John and Carol Taylor

Rev. Peter Mansfield

Mrs Maureen Kearney

Mrs Brown

Paul Downey

Brides at Bestman

Dexter Wansel

Sr. Julia Bolton, Hermit of the Holy Family

Fr. John Zagrella O'Pream

in memory of James Ernest Hardy

The Authors

JAD ADAMS is an independent historian working as a television producer and author. His books include *Madder Music, Stronger Wine: The Life of Ernest Dowson,* (2000) and *Hideous Absinthe: A History of the Devil in a Bottle* (2004). He has also written biographies of Tony Benn, Emmeline Pankhurst, Rudyard Kipling and of the Nehru-Gandhi dynasty. His television work includes biographies of Kitchener, of Bill and Hillary Clinton, and of characters from London's East End. He is a Fellow of the Royal Historical Society and is Chair of the Croydon-based homelessness charity, Nightwatch.

GERRY COLL was born in Camberwell, London, in 1961, and was educated at Shirley Oaks Primary School and St. Mary's RC High School. In the early 80s he became a founder member of Croydon Association for the Young Single Homeless, CAYSH. A qualified Community and Youth worker, he has a Diploma in Pastoral Work (Commendation) and an RSA Certificate in Counselling Skills in the development of learning and an Access Diploma in Psychodynamic Counselling. He works for a local authority.

The previous book jointly written by these authors was *The History of Shirley Oaks Children's Home.*

Contents

Illustrations

Front cover photograph by courtesy of London Borough of Bexley.
Back cover line illustraion by Gillian Richie.

* *Photographs reproduced by kind permission of*
The London Metropolitan Archives.

Foreword

The Hollies at Sidcup was originally a villa in the countryside beyond London. But from 1902 to 1989 it was the site of an extensive children's home, run on behalf of urban public authorities from London itself. There had been a pattern from the early 19th century onwards of residential schools and homes being built just outside London by Poor Law authorities, often representing groups of civil parishes collaborating for the purpose. It was the dissolution in 1902 of one such collaborative scheme, the South Metropolitan District Schools at Brighton Road in Sutton, which prompted the building of the institution discussed in this book. The Greenwich and Deptford Board of Guardians in south-east London had been one of the contributors to the schools at Sutton, and upon the announcement of the schools' intended closure, they bought the 62-acre site at The Hollies in order to build the Sidcup Children's Homes in 1901-2. This was therefore an exact parallel with the case of Shirley Oaks Children's Home near Croydon, which was opened by the St. Olave's or Bermondsey Board of Guardians in 1903 and which was the subject of a previous book by Jad Adams and Gerry Coll.

The Poor Law still existed in 1902 and it continued to be administered by boards of guardians until 1930. The Greenwich and Deptford board remained the authority at The Hollies in those years. Then the London County Council took over. When that authority in turn ceased to exist, in 1965, The Hollies came under the control of the London Borough of Southwark. This is a pattern repeated – with local variations – many times elsewhere. The naming of the home changed also. The London County Council renamed it the Lamorbey Residential School in 1930, and did not actually use the name of The Hollies for the whole site until 1950.

It is well to remember that different views of what was appropriate in the care of children prevailed in different eras. In 1902, for example, many boys were sent to training ships for eventual service in the Royal Navy or in the Merchant Marine, or to Canada, for what would usually have been hard manual work on remote farms; and girls from Poor Law homes were largely destined for domestic service. All these things were normal then; but they seem unthinkable now. It has to be remembered that as the children were either orphans or were effectively without their own homes and families, they needed residential work when they left The Hollies at 14 or 15. They could not be wholly self-sufficient at that age.

Historians always have to be careful not to attribute one era's ideas (and criticisms) to another. The beginning of the 20th century was the heyday of 'cottage homes', a reaction against very large, barrack-like Victorian institutions. The idea was to make the place approximate to a normal home, with foster-parents presiding over a house. It is interesting to read here, however, that even then there were contrary views. The authors quote Lord Crewe, a Liberal politician of the time, who spoke out in favour of the 'scattered homes' that Camberwell operated – Poor Law houses scattered amidst normal, family-occupied houses – as opposed to isolated places such as The Hollies, however carefully they were planned. Lord Crewe's opinion was unusual, for there were many apparently admiring visitors to The Hollies in its early days, often from overseas. The Lord Mayor of London visited in 1904, a sterling mark of approval.

A surprising phase of the home's history was its large Jewish contingent in the 1930s and 1940s, following the closure of Stepney Jewish Children's Home in 1934. Up to a quarter of the children were Jewish just before the Second World War.

Of the 62 acres at the site, 40 were taken up by a farm. Self-sufficiency was the aim, as on a country estate of the time. Until the late 1930s, there was also a school just for the children on the site; later, they attended ordinary schools elsewhere. In the early days the site was very isolated from the rest of the world. 'Bang went the gates behind us', wrote a woman who became an inmate at the beginning of the First World War.

It was decidedly harsh to keep brothers and sisters permanently apart, and harsh to allow visitors only briefly once a month. In the 1920s, one of the guardians reported here sounds remarkably like the 'gentleman in a white waistcoat' in Dickens's *Oliver Twist* in his relentless pursuit of savings. The advent of the London County Council's responsibility in 1930 appears to have improved the regime considerably, but some children's memoirs of later years still reflect a clear harshness from individuals on the staff. After about 1950, however, there seems to have been a gradual loss of control, leading eventually to a local feeling that the home was a hotbed of crime. The memoir of a former member of staff is little short of an admission of despair in controlling the home, an extraordinary reversal of what had applied half a century before.

The events in the autumn of 1983, when the home was forcibly emptied and needlessly damaged in the wake of a trade union dispute involving the staff, amounted to little less than the sack of The Hollies. Whatever were they thinking of? Quite clearly, they were not thinking of the children. It was an extraordinary and disgraceful denouement to an 80-year history which had certainly always been sad but which had undoubtedly been well-meaning for the most part. The authors merit our gratitude for recording an institution that played such a large part in the lives of so many people.

Stephen Humphrey
January 2005

Preface

This book documents The Hollies – A Home for Children. From the beginning the home was known as 'The Sidcup Homes.' The site changed names a number of times during the first half of the twentieth century so it is also referred to as the Greenwich and Deptford Homes and as the Lamorbey Homes.

Although the Hollies buildings are located in Sidcup, it was originally built by the Greenwich and Deptford Board of Guardians, who administered the Home from 1902 to 1930. This book is a commentary on aspects of the care system of the twentieth century and also a part of the history of Bexley.

I hope the people who read this will find it illuminating and interesting, giving insight into the lives of generations of children that resided there. I feel that life in the Home was a microcosm, a reflection of the society that existed outside the boundaries of the establishment. Earlier events and discipline that happened inside the institution may seem harsh or even cruel by today's standards but were perhaps no worse than one might have experienced at a boarding school of that era. The story has to be understood in the context of the social conditions that existed then.

For much of last century, staff had little training. One of the most significant aspects regarding residential child care was that staff were not given professional guidance on managing young people in their care. Staff adopted their own practices and beliefs, either born out of their own upbringing and experiences or maybe because they believed children in their care should be treated differently to other children.

The book touches on some sensitive and emotive issues, which have been reported in some detail by the media locally and nationally over many years. They are included for their historical significance. This book has brought together information from a number of sources including personal accounts by a number of people who spent part of or all of their childhood there. Their accounts are seen through the senses, experiences and perceptions of children who lived there, in one case almost a century ago. These children have managed to climb above the adversity, obstacles and barriers that have been placed in front of them. They retain the copyright to their own accounts. To protect the identity of some children, forenames only have been used in the narrative.

Many people have pre-conceived ideas as to why children are put into care. In the latter part of the Hollies' history as a children's home as seen here, there was a tendency to judge the children who resided there, and paint them all with the same brush. Many came into care through no fault of their own – yet felt stigmatised and discriminated against. Some children even felt that they were affected by mistreatment, discrimination and institutionalised racism whilst in care. Sometimes people believe that such children must have done something fundamentally wrong.

The story of this children's home ends with the events surrounding the industrial action centring on pay and conditions taken nationally by residential social workers in the autumn of 1983. Residential workers as late as the 1970s had no fixed working week. They were seen as permanent carers. Unlike 'in the field' social workers, who were required to have a certificate in social work (CQSW), or at least working towards one under supervision, residential workers could work with children, having no qualifications. Staff were not police checked but were required to sign a disclaimer stating that they had no previous criminal offences. Only a handful of staff had the equivalent of the residential qualification, Children in Residential Care and the Care of Young People (CRCYP). Some residential staff saw themselves as the Cinderella of the childcare system and were routinely expected to work overtime. The main casualties at The Hollies were the young people. Instead of being treated as vulnerable subjects in public care, they were handled like objects and many of them were forcibly removed like furniture in a house clearance.

I asked Jad Adams to use his expertise in archive research to prise out historical information from the files in the London Metropolitan Archives and I am grateful to him for putting his skills to this use, for supplying historical fragments from this source and giving historical interpretations where relevant. The overall concept and interpretation of this book is, however, my own. Equally, it is left to the reader to draw his or her own observations and conclusions, especially to the historical context of this publication.

With little material available about the Poor Law as it related to children, and in the absence of any other detailed historical publion the Hollies as a children's home, I trust this book will be of value. I hope the residents of Bexley find it interesting. Some aspects of the book have been complex to write. By writing this account my intention is to provide an impartial and balanced history of the Home as well as providing an authentic and clear historical record.

I am often asked what is the purpose of writing a book on this subject. The reason is I have learned from my own experience that sometimes you have to make sense of the past in order to make sense of the present.

Gerry Coll

1

The South Metropolitan District Schools

The proponents of the Poor Law Amendment Act of 1834 chiefly aimed to save money in the care of the poor, and one of their principal means was to create unions of parishes, which would set up a single workhouse for each union. In a similar vein, a parliamentary committee recommended in 1837 that schools should be set up which would be shared by Poor Law authorities. Just as there were now 'union workhouses', it was thought there should be 'district schools.' They were duly established in London in the late 1840s.

Before 1834, parishes had often supplemented their workhouses with special provision elsewhere for children. Parishes within the present London Borough of Southwark had sent infants to be nursed, and older children to be educated, to establishments well outside their boundaries. The parish of St. Mary Magdalen, Bermondsey, for example, leased Church House at Merton between 1820 and 1845 for use as the Bermondsey Infant Establishment. This was an institution wholly run by and for one parish, but there were also contract schools, which served several parishes. A well-known example was F. G. Aubin's School of Industry or Proprietary Poor Law School at Westow Hill in Lower or West Norwood. In 1849 Mr Aubin's establishment was taken over as the first premises of the Central London District Schools, to which St. Saviour's Union in Southwark subscribed. These schools removed in 1856 into purpose-built premises at Hanwell, west of London.

The South Metropolitan School District was formed by an order of the Poor Law Board on 12 March, 1849. The constituent authorities were the parishes of St. Mary Magdalen, Bermonsdsey, and St. Mary, Rotherhithe, and St. Olave's Union, which was itself an amalgamation of St. Olave's, St. John's and St. Thomas's Parishes in Southwark. Permanent buildings were ready several years later. Land was bought at Sutton in 1851, where the Brighton Road School was built and occupied by 1855. It lasted until the dissolution of the district in 1902, with many additions and extensions after 1855. Further buildings were acquired at Herne Bay (Kent) in 1876, Witham (in Essex) in 1882 (for use by orphans), and Banstead Road (also at Sutton) in 1884. The property at Brighton Road was by far the biggest, comprising 92 acres. The remaining three totalled 28 acres between them. Many other authorities were added to the original sponsors: Camberwell, Greenwich, Newington, Woolwich and Stepney all subscribed for varying periods.

In 1891-2, the schools were supported by no fewer than seventeen parishes, which represented a population of 695,577. The average number of children in all the premises was 2,238, of whom 1,327 were housed in the Brighton Road School. Expenditure in the year was £58,732, making a weekly cost for each child of ten shillings eleven pence, but of only nine shillings threepence at Brighton Road School.

A well-known leather manufacturer from the Grange in Bermondsey, James Garnar, who represented St. Olave's Union among the District's managers, wrote a report on the schools in March, 1892. He deliberately emphasized that in this Poor Law institution, an Oliver Twist might ask for more: 'and those who are blessed with a stronger appetite than others may come up for a second helping, so long as any is left to be served'.

District Schools were a product of the early years of the New Poor Law. By the end of the 19th century attitudes had changed. There was a feeling that schools should not be so large. The Local Government Board declared in 1897 that the South Metropolitan District Schools had inadequate accommodation and recommended their dissolution but this did not take place finally until 29 September, 1902. Long before then, the constituent authorities had begun to plan for their replacement. St. Olave's Union set up a Schools (Shirley) Committee in January, 1898, which planned the Shirley Schools near Croydon that were opened in 1903. Similarly, the Greenwich Union planned what was to be The Hollies, the subject of this book. The buildings of the South Metropolitan District Schools were bought and taken over by the Metropolitan Asylums Board.

Children in Care Before 1900

The Poor Law under which the children's home referred to here was administered dated back to 1834. This established workhouses in which the destitute poor would be kept in conditions worse than the worst they might experience outside the workhouse. The objective was to ensure that only those who really needed help would go there; the administrators of the Poor Law did not want the 'idle poor' living in luxury on the rates.

It was recognised that there was a problem with the workhouse child, who could hardly be held responsible for his or her poverty. Left in the workhouse, moreover, these children were felt to develop the bad habits of their elders. Large, barrack-like 'schools' were therefore set up from the late 1840s in which thousands of children would live together.

School Districts were set up in 1849 by order of the Poor Law Board, to administer the schools for these child paupers. In the case of the home studied here, the authority involved was the South Metropolitan School District which eventually took children from the parishes of Bermondsey, Rotherhithe, Camberwell, Greenwich, Newington, Woolwich and Stepney.

The school in Brighton Road, Sutton, whence came the children who first populated the Sidcup home, was built in 1852-55 and was occupied until 1902.

The Industrial Schools and Reformatory Schools Acts of 1854 and 1857 permitted schools to be set up for children who had offended or were in danger of doing so. Reformatory schools aimed at 'correcting' crime. Industrial schools aimed at preventing crime by caring for the neglected before they became delinquent by giving them an honest trade by which to earn their living. Clearly this is the origin of the 'industrial training' which will be documented in the school examined here.

For most of the nineteenth century the Poor Law administrators had to provide for destitute or deserted children, or those whose parents were in the workhouse. They had no responsibility for children living in their own homes, however neglected or abused they might be. Acts of Parliament of 1889 and 1899 gave the Poor Law Guardians the right to assume parental rights in the case of neglect and the Prevention of Cruelty to Children Act later extended this.

These Acts gave legal backing to the attitude of mind which said children must be 'rescued' from the family and conditions which might lead them to a life of vice. Hence the efforts which, it will be seen, were made to keep children from their families and previous habitats, including severely restricting visiting from relatives, and having the institutions built far out of towns.

By the end of the nineteenth century the Local Government Board, which now had overall responsibility for the administration of the Poor Law, was coming in for increasing criticism of its 'barrack' children's homes which were really nothing but children's workhouses. A report of the Poor Law Schools Committee of 1896 was against the large schools. Eventually the Local Government Board declared in 1897 that the School Districts would be abolished and the local unions must make provision for their own children.

Criticisms of the earlier system were well taken but reforming efforts foundered on the question of which alternative to adopt. Experiments had been taking place in the private sector in Britain, France and Germany to establish more humane homes for pauper children. Dr Barnardo's homes for boys were based on large scale communal living but when the same system was tried for girls it was totally unsuccessful, for all discipline broke down. The solution was to adopt an idea pioneered by Thomas Stephenson and have the Barnardo's girls in small groups in cottages with a surrogate mother and father in charge.

In 1878 the Local Government Board had looked at five innovative homes run by voluntary organisations aiming 'to bring up destitute or criminal children in habits of religion and virtue.' These included The Homes for Little Boys at Farningham, Kent; Dr Barnardo's Village Home for Girls, Ilford; and Princess Mary's Village Home, Addlestone. Most, if not all, the elements were present in these homes that were incorporated into the children's homes such as the Sidcup Homes (later The Hollies) which were built at the beginning of the next century. There were children in smallish groups in cottages on what was called the 'family system'; a house mother for each, with widows chosen for preference, 'as best calculated to gain the hearts of the children, and to represent the nearest approach to the natural mothers'; and training so the children would be able to earn an honest living on departure.

Sidcup Before the Children's Home

Local historians Katherine Harding and Denise Baldwin in their book *The Early Beginnings* (2003) noted, 'The first reference to Sidcup as a place name for the area occurred in 1254, during the reign of Henry II. Over the years various spellings have been used, including Sikecoppe, Cetecoppe, Sedecoppe and Sedcop and it was not until the 18th century that Sidcup became the generally accepted spelling. The name would appear to derive from the Anglo-Saxon: 'sette' meaning flat and 'coppe' meaning hill; hence Sidcup means 'a flat hill top'.

'Until relatively recently, Sidcup, Lamorbey, and Halfway Street were quite separate rural communities. It was only with the arrival of the railways firm that the area started to develop into the present urban community. The railway came to Sidcup in 1866 with the construction of the Dartford Loop Line and the line was electrified in 1926. An indication of the speed with which the area changed can be gauged from the fact that the population increased between 1871 and 1911 from 390 to 8,493 people! This compares with the present population of more than 50,000.'

'The great sweep of British history seems to have passed Sidcup by, however. We can boast of no great statesmen, military leaders, literary giants or famous scientists; no battles or other major events took place in or near to Sidcup (although, some recent graduates from the Rose Bruford College of Performing Arts have appeared in television dramas). In a historical sense though, probably the most famous resident of Sidcup was Dame Ethel Smyth, a distinguished composer and leading member of the suffragette movement, who was born in the now demolished Sidcup House, in 1858.'

The Hollies mansion which would form part of the children's home was built between 1744 and 1748, on the site of a medieval manor house. The earliest reference to a building on this site, in Sidcup, Kent, comes from a 1769 map, which has a Marrowbone Hall here, later called Bone Hall. By 1842 it was renamed The Holly's and was owned by Thomas Lewin. The first appearance of the name The Hollies comes in 1847.

The building was later pulled down and rebuilt nearby around 1857. This is the building which is still standing. The red bricks and steep gables are its most prominent features. It is recorded as being occupied by a family called Brown from at least 1861 until 1882. The heads of household named are first Thomas, then Harry Brown. Just before the end of the nineteenth century, Sir George Woodman from Mottingham is recorded as living there. He sold the land and property to the Board of Guardians of the Greenwich Poor Law Union who retained the building called The Hollies when the children's home was built, and used it as the administrative block.

The Greenwich Workhouse c.1905.

2

Building the Homes

The architect for the Sidcup Homes was Thomas Dinwiddy (1845-1928), who practised in Greenwich from 1866 until 1902 though he continued to advise on major projects. He was made a Fellow of the Royal Institute of British Architects in 1909. Among his major public buildings were the Roan School for Girls in Devonshire Drive, Greenwich, 1877-8; the Jubilee Almshouses in Greenwich High Road of 1888; New Cross Baths in Laurie Grove built in 1895-8; and Greenwich Workhouse in Marvels Lane, Grove Park, built in 1902-4.

The Sidcup Children's Homes were built in 1901, Dinwiddy working with his son Thomas Norman. The development was illustrated in the *Architect's Journal* of 12 July 1901. The first builders chosen, W. Pattinson & Sons, could do the job cheaply but wanted 18 months while the Guardians wanted the work finished in a year, so the job was given to Thomas Rowbotham of Birmingham, who had recently built Grove Park Workhouse for the Guardians. They were very proud of this building and had sent a drawing of it to be displayed at the Paris Exhibition of 1900, as an example of municipal excellence. Rowbotham charged £107,777. The Guardians would raise the money with a loan which would take 60 years to pay back.

They enunciated their philosophy, 'to bring up the children as to fit them to enter on the struggle for existence with some at any rate of the advantages which children of the more favoured members of the community enjoyed.'

The Guardians' architect supplied a set of drawings on 26 April 1900 and the plans were referred to the buildings committee for an estimate on costs. The specification was for accommodation for 400 children but the plans were drawn up for 524, which was more usually the number of children who were present, on the site of 62 acres. As well as the accommodation there was to be a school house, a laundry and wash house, swimming baths, 'gas making and distributing

THE SIDCUP HOMES 1900–01

An artist's reconstruction of one of the cottages.

A ground-floor plan.

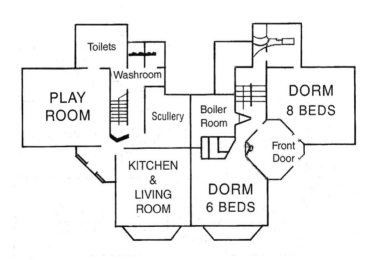

8

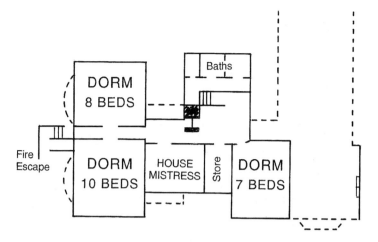

From the original plans of one of the boys' homes:
First floor (above) and ground floor (below).

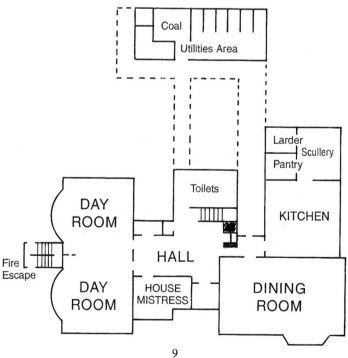

9

Children's Homes at Sidcup c.1901 provided by Greenwich Poor Law Union.
Artist's impression.

apparatus, a gymnasium and a well and pumping machine'. The 62-acre site would also contain stables and a farm.

The boys' houses were called The Beeches, The Firs, The Limes and The Oaks. These three-storey buildings housed 50 boys each. There were thirteen twinned cottages for girls also named after trees. They were Maple, Lilac, Laurel, Laburnum, Hazel, Hawthorne, Elm, Elders, Chestnut, Cedar, Almond, Acacia, Mulberry, Myrtle, Olive, Palm, Pine, Poplar, Rowan and Sycamore. Willow and Walnut Cottages each accommodated 12 boys of infants. Additionally there was The Hollies, the administrative building and accommodation for senior staff, which later gave its name to the whole complex.

A married couple was to reside in each of the four blocks for 50 boys, to act as foster parents. The male officers were experienced tradesmen, who would teach the boys a trade. In addition two assistant foster mothers would help in each of these larger homes. A foster mother was placed 'in charge' of each of the homes for girls and infants. The infirmary would be under the charge of a nurse and contained 29 beds.

The estimated and annual charges for the maintenance and upkeep of the large establishment were about £30,000. Calculated on the basis of the Homes being fully occupied, and exclusive of loan repayments, the total cost of the land and buildings was more than £160,000.

The Homes were under the jurisdiction of the Board of Guardians of the Greenwich Union and so were often referred to as Greenwich Children's Homes. From the start they were formally called Sidcup Children's Homes and later referred to as Sidcup Residential School. When the London County Council took over in 1930 the establishment was renamed Lamorbey Residential School. It became The Hollies in 1950 and was officially closed in 1989.

The foundation stone was laid on 15 April 1901 and the opening ceremony was intended to be a grand affair but expectations exceeded results. First the Prince of Wales was asked but he was unable to come. The Duke of Fife was then asked but he also declined. Going down the social hierarchy, the MP Lord Hugh Cecil was asked but he also turned them down, so they just had a minimal ceremony with the Guardians themselves and their friends on 30 October 1902, when the homes were already running.

After the singing of the 'Old Hundreth', and prayers by the Rev. W.

Boys outside The Beeches, The Firs, The Limes, and The Oaks, c.1903.

Horon, the architect, Mr T. Dinwiddy, handed to Mr J. P. Lewis, Chairman of the Building Committee, a gold key of the buildings, which he handed to Mr J. E. Morton, Chairman of the Board of Guardians, who, having welcomed the company, made reference to criticisms which had been passed on the action of the Board in erecting these homes.

The Guardians, he said, did not embark on the scheme with light hearts – it was forced upon them by the decision of the Local Government Board to disband the Sutton Schools – a decision in which the Guardians had no voice whatever – the necessity was cast on them for providing, not for the education merely, but for the housing, feeding, clothing and general maintenance of over 500 children. The Guardians had made every enquiry to find a suitable building within a reasonable distance of the Union, but without success. It became more obvious that the only method of complying with the requirements of the Local Government Board was to acquire a site and build a sufficient number of homes.

Morton was underlining in his keynote speech a fact which is important to remember in looking at the history of the Hollies: Poor Law provision was always a contested area of public policy. Individuals involved in the provision, both elected and appointed, had their own views about child care and sought to impose them on the system as best they could. Benign and well-informed criticism of the provision made at children's homes was ever-present, alongside official neglect and indifference.

In a report to the Poor Law Board an inspector wrote in these early years: 'The monotonous and confined life of the children who, when orphan or deserted, live in the schools continuously, must to a great extent prevent the development of many of those faculties of mind and body which in the case of children who must look forward to a hard industrial life, it is most important to expand. Anything therefore which will relieve this monotony and bring them into closer connection with the outside world is to be welcomed.' Some of the more enlightened Boards of Guardians did make efforts to bring some breath of the outside world into the children's lives, but on the whole the children remained segregated from the rest of the community, living their lives in isolation and knowing little or nothing of the world around them.

Such big children's homes as that built at Sidcup remained contro-

View of the infants' and girls' cottages in the late stages of construction, seen from the Water Tower, c.1902.

versial. An organisation named the State Children's Association was against 'rearing children in masses'. Its chairman, Lord Crewe, argued that 'the disadvantages of these village communities are many and grave. The children are isolated from the ordinary life of their class and are enveloped by pauper association and influence. The artificial ready-made life inseparable from these communities seriously unfits the children for contending with the difficulties of real life' and the buildings and staff 'makes pauperism attractive to parents desirous of shirking their responsibilities.'

Lord Crewe criticised the Greenwich Board of Guardians for setting up homes like Sidcup and by contrast praised Camberwell which, 'having 560 children to provide for, has hired 30 houses in the parish, each accommodating about 10 children, and has thus already provided for 328 of those chargeable . . . without enormous capital expenditure, and with the great additional advantages that (1) the children are not kept as a class apart, but mix in play, at school and at church with the children of the district; (2) they are no longer ostensibly pauper children; (3) and are more fitted by the training of natural family life to meet their own difficulties and temptations.

Lord Crewe urged careful investigation into the circumstances of each child's coming into the care of the Poor Law. He advised a number of different solutions tailored to individual children such as outboarding with what would later be considered foster families; small Poor Law homes; training ships (for training for the Navy) and emigration to Canada.

While Lord Crewe's view of the large homes was eventually to become the prevailing one, there were many who were prepared to defend the system. The *Kentish Mercury* of 25 February 1910 reported a Mr Bardsley comparing the boarding-out system with the homes to the advantage of the homes. 'The weekly cost per head at Sidcup had been reduced from 18 shillings 1 penny to 15 shillings four-and-a-half-pence and he emphasised the fact that the latter sum included the cost of the premises and of education, a very considerable sum.'

One reaction by the Guardians to the continued criticism of their work was to make it as small a drain on the public purse as possible. The Poor Law Guardians of every location were obsessed with itemised bills and there are impressive tables of comparative cost between the different institutions. Block schools could, however, be run far more cheaply if the Guardians had a mind to do so; the cheapest in the league was one of these, run by Islington, and costing 9s.7d. (48p) per child per week.

There were frequent visits by foreigners, often Germans or Americans, who wanted to look over the establishment. There were also visits by institutions like the Children's Aid Society, the Band of Hope, the South Place Ethical Society and the Amalgamated Society of Engineers. The Guardians officially encouraged scrutiny or at least did not discourage it. This implies they considered they were running a model institution.

The Staff and Daily Life

The staff were to be headed by a Master of Homes for Boys at £100 per year. His job description said he had to be aged between 28 and 45 and to have had experience in a Poor Law institution. Joseph Steer was appointed. His counterpart, Miss Ada Mitchell, was a Matron of Homes for Girls and Infants with the same experience requirement and an age of 28–40 at a wage of £70 per year. In the end it turned out that these jobs were combined with those of Headmaster and Headmistress. The Headmaster would admit boys, 'cause them to be cleansed. Properly clothed and sent to their respective Homes'. He would look after the cleanliness of homes, discipline, diet and Industrial Training. The Headmistress would do a similar job for the girls' homes.

The other senior post was filled by Harry Longhurst, the Clerk and Steward, responsible for the stores, farm, engineering, laundry and the fabric of the buildings, and who was paid £100 a year. There was also a needlemistress, a storekeeper, a cook, and a band and drill instructor. A medical officer, Dr Henry A. Duffett, would come every morning before 10. The Guardians provided the drugs for him to prescribe and he received £100. There were 30 foster mothers appointed in 1902. They received £24 a year and a uniform. Of these 27 were unmarried and it may well have been that the other three were widows, for no mention is made of their husbands.

There were also couples of foster parents, presumably caring for the infants. These were chosen very carefully so the husband could also teach boys a trade in the 'industrial training' side of the home. The four couples were: a carpenter, William Turner, and his wife Rebecca; shoemaker Henry Girling and Elizabeth Girling; tailor Paul Hows and his wife Mary; and a gardener called H. H. Davies living

The staff of Sidcup Homes, early 1900s.

with a Miss Evelyn M. Elliott. Perhaps these last two were elderly or related to each other.

Other staff were a housemaid, kitchen maid, servants to the Headmaster and Headmistress, porters and laundry workers. Staff were expected to keep to strict rules, such as that forbidding alcohol on the site. When a foster mother at The Limes, Mrs Wilson, was recommended by her doctor to take stout daily, she had to receive permission from the Board to do so. Staff in their one and a half days off a fortnight had to be booked back in by the gate keeper before 10pm or the head of the home was informed.

Foster mothers had a dark striped dress covered by an apron for use in the mornings and a black serge dress for the afternoons. Later, the afternoon uniform was changed to a navy blue frock. The girls at the homes would wear a navy blue striped dress for weekdays and for Sunday a heavy navy blue serge in smock style gathered front and back. There were three buttons down the back with a hook at the top with long gathered sleeves with white lace around the neck.

Children were up at 6am but this was modified to 6.30 in dark weather. There would be prayers before breakfast (and after tea). Other rules were that children must wash three times a day and be bathed at least once a week. Baths had to be not less than 88 degrees Fahrenheit and not more than 98 degrees. Their hair must be combed once a day. They were all to be taught to wash, sweep and dust, and girls to set a table.

At the gates of Greenwich and Deptford Homes, early 1900s.

Foster mothers were told, 'You will take an interest in the children's play and recreation as much as possible . . . you will not allow a child to read pernicious literature on any account.' From the start children were not permitted to go outside the grounds of the home, and only the cricket team ever went out or occasionally a child with a pass would be allowed to run an errand for the foster mother.

Children could be visited on the first Wednesday of every month between six and seven but could have no more than two friends visiting at a time. Children were forbidden to visit their parents during holidays.

There would be daily drill practice for the boys and frequent trips to the swimming bath, probably for both sexes (though separately). The Head Master complained to the Board that their policy of draining and re-filling the swimming bath only once a week led to 'a quite unacceptable amount of sediment to be seen'.

It was after one such swimming trip that the Headmaster wrote, 'I very much regret to have to report the first death at the Homes.' It was on 2 August 1906 when George Coombes, who had been in the Homes for two years, returned from swimming and was laughing and joking as he lined up with the others outside the door of his house (The Beeches) then suddenly he fell down unconscious. He was taken to the infirmary where they tried to dose him with brandy and sent for the doctor but by the time he came the child was dead. An inquest said he had died of a small fracture at the base of his skull – presumably he had hit his head and thought nothing of it but it had formed a blood clot that killed him. His service at Bexley Cemetery was attended by a small contingent of playmates and his sister, also in the Homes, and his mother from Greenwich Workhouse.

Two years later a boy called Ernest Compart fell 28 feet out of one of the windows in the early hours of the morning. He was conscious when taken to the infirmary and he said he had jumped out of the window because he had heard screams. The least sinister explanation is that he had a nightmare. He died five hours after his fall. The Headmaster recommended that all windows should be shut at night but the Guardians, trusting to a belief in the beneficial effects of fresh air insisted that the windows of all bedrooms, 'should be kept open at least two inches'.

Education

The school's Headmaster (and Master of Homes for Boys), Joseph Steer, wrote record books from 1902–14, which are the only personal document which survives in the archives to describe day to day life at the Homes.

The Headmistress (and Matron of Homes for Girls and Infants) was Miss Ada Mitchell. There were three male and four female assistant teachers and two female teachers for the infants.

The children were taught reading, writing, arithmetic, geography, history, elementary science, grammar, advanced drawing, geometry 'and possibly elementary algebra for the brighter lads'. There was manual training for the boys and cookery and dressmaking for girls.

The schools inspector in September 1904, 'found the necessary number of children under instruction in the needle room, laundry, shoemaker's shop, tailor's shop, carpenter's shop, garden and bake house'.

In 1906 the inspector's report said 'there is too much mechanical work in the girls' arithmetic and not enough attempt to give the children an intelligent grasp of the methods they are employing'.

The school had a library and a small museum. Both of these attracted contributions from visitors and well-wishers. A visitor, for example, gave them samples of ore from California. Students from

Goldsmiths College and Avery Hill College visited regularly, to gain teaching practice and do demonstration lessons.

In July 1909 a Miss Foofitt, infants' teacher, was reprimanded for breaking the rules with regard to corporal punishment. Clearly, the rules of the Homes were enforced on staff.

Health

The Homes had their own infirmary, where there would generally be ten or fewer children. The Homes also had an ambulance that had been purchased for £11.12s.4d (£11.62p). The danger of epidemics in such a closed community was so great that if there were scarlet fever in Sidcup, all children were forbidden to leave the grounds of the Homes. When one case was diagnosed the boy, Thomas Howard, was taken to the Brook Hospital in Greenwich and his home, The Oaks, was isolated with children there permitted no contact with other children until it was clear they were not infected.

The Medical Officer reported in 1904, 'up to the present I have extracted a large number of teeth but these, with four or five exceptions, have been much decayed and aching. The exceptions were for teeth which were brought to my attention as being abnormal and disfiguring.' He recommended that this work be done in future by a dentist so the services of one were secured at the cost of £50 a year.

Arrangements were made for Henry Dunn & Co to carry out funerals of children at £2.14s. (£2. 70p).

Discipline

Foster mothers were told, in their rules, which were printed on 17 July 1902, 'You are not to inflict corporal punishment, or to confine a child to a dark room, or to deprive it of its food. It is desirable to control the children in a kind and firm manner rather than by severity. Set a good example yourself, and check all small faults. Train the children in habits of industry, cleanliness, honesty, thrift, civility and self-reliance.'

One stricture if children did not behave themselves was to be sent back to the workhouse. This was the fate of Emily Miller, 'against whom several charges of theft have been proved', on 9 April 1903.

Corporal punishment was rare and when it was used it was regulated: the level of punishment and the misdemeanour were reported to the Children's Home Committee, at first in the head teacher's report book, and later in a separate punishment book. This has not survived, but months pass with no recorded punishment in the early period, when the reports formed part of the head's main report, so we can judge that Joseph Steer was not heavy with the cane. One typical report is of Henry Taylor, aged 13, who in December 1902, 'got through the scullery window in The Firs and stole some apples. He was punished with six strokes of the cane.'

The Punishment Book for the Homes was kept as a record of what punishment had been administered to boys who misbehaved. Samples of offences and beatings are recorded here for public record. With names removed, they are:

1903: Rudeness to foster mother – three stripes with cane. Running away – six stripes with cane. Misbehaviour in dormitory – four stripes with cane.

1906: Disobedience in school – three strokes. Misbehaviour in dormitory – four strokes. Disobedience – three strokes. Theft – six strokes.

1911: Very troublesome – several small taps with cane. Stubborn and disobedient – two strokes with cane. Naughty boy – two strokes; Impertinent age 12 – three strokes.

1919: Rudeness to foster mother – four strokes. Out of bounds – two strokes. Display of bad temper – two strokes.

1947: Continued absconding – four smacks on buttocks.

1952: Truant from school – two strokes on buttocks. Continued absconding after repeated warning – two strokes on buttocks.

1961: Striking and biting a schoolteacher – two strokes. Repeatedly breaking windows after warning – two strokes on buttocks.

1965: Striking housemother – four strokes with slipper. Throwing fireworks into Firs Kitchen – three strokes with cane. Persistent disobedience to foster mother – two strokes.

1972: Breaking windows – four strokes.

This shows that before the Second World War discipline was strictly maintained so that the sort of behaviour which would merit punishment was general naughtiness. By the 1960s and 70s punishment was reserved for very bad behaviour, amounting to assault or criminal damage.

Religion

The day was structured with religion. There was a short prayer on rising and prayers at breakfast – grace was said before and after each meal. School opened with the Lord's Prayer and a familiar reading from scripture. School closed with a hymn and the Lord's Prayer. There were then prayers at teatime and a prayer at bedtime.

On Sundays there would be a service for the children conducted by a visiting clergyman. There would be Sunday school morning and afternoon. Brothers and sisters were allowed to sit together in church.

Entertainment would often be of a religious nature: Mr Cecil Pitman gave a series of Lantern Lectures (smoked glass slides) on five successive Wednesday evenings in 1903 on the subject of Missionary Work. The Religious Trust Society kept them supplied with tracts.

A major controversy on the Board of Guardians was whether children entered as 'Church of England' in the school register should be taken to services conducted by Non-conformist clergy and lay people. The vote on this was close, with the motion to retain the current approach won by 11 to 10.

Dress and Diet

All boys had a tweed suit at seven shillings and sixpence (37p though of course the value of money was far greater then so there is no direct comparison) and a cap at four pence. Most clothes were made on site, however. The Homes had a jersey-making machine and a stocking machine and made many more of their own clothes in the tailor's shop and the needlework room.

Girls had a dark navy striped dress for weekdays, for Sundays a heavy navy serge in a smock-style gathered front and back, with three buttons down the back, with a hook at the top, long gathered sleeves, with white lace round the neck. The material was very rough, grey lining inside the bodice. A white pinafore was always worn over the dress. Navy cloaks with hoods were worn to school. Navy coats, with straw hats in the summer, were worn on Sundays. Laced up boots were worn for school with shoes for Sunday wear. The housemother and children would knit the children's stockings in the house. The children each had to have three pairs, and spares were knitted and kept in stock so a great deal of sock knitting had to be done. There was also clothing for wearing in the sickbay.

The amounts of food provided for the children were strictly regulated. The weekly quantities per child were, in ounces:

bread 112;	peas 2;	cocoa 3;
oatmeal 4;	potatoes 42;	tea;
flour 12;	vegetables 14	jam or marmalade 4;
butter 3;	bacon 2;	treacle 4;
1 egg;	milk 140;	fruit 4;
sugar 7;	meat (uncooked and	currants or raisins 2.
rice 3;	reckoned free from bone) 20;	

It was, therefore, a vitamin-enriched pauper's diet with the bulk of calories coming from bread and potatoes. The high level of meat is not remarkable for the time; low quality meat was not expensive and even the poor had long been used to eating meat daily. Much of the produce, like the fresh milk, would have come from the farm. The older boys grew vegetables on the farm; and eggs were produced on the premises too, as there were 36 hens, but the birds themselves were eaten only by the chief officers.

On Saturday 24 June 1904, the Lord Mayor of London (Sir T. H. Richie, MP) and the Lady Mayoress, Miss Richie (his daughter) visited the Homes. The Mayor said it had given him the greatest pleasure to come down there, and to see the admirable manner in which everything connected with the Homes was carried out.

Recreation

As befits a school with a swimming bath, Sidcup Childrens' Homes were successful in the Poor Law Schools' Swimming Competition. In 1904, Benjamin Boswell received the first prize for Plunging and John Carpenter the same for Graceful Diving. The football team entered for the Greenwich Schools Trophy and won it once, in 1918. In 1907 the cricket team won the Westminster shield at the Oval. The same year the band won a cup at the Crystal Palace which was awarded at the Homes by Mr W. I. Henry Iles, the founder of the band competition.

The children entered flower arrangements for the 'Wild Flower

Show' of the Sidcup Scientific Society. There would be outings, like the Lamorbey Sunday School Treat to Bognor on which the boys of the band were invited to go. The editor of the religious magazine *Truth* provided gifts of toys and a sixpence each for the children at Christmas time. The smallest children would receive a penny.

Admission and Discharge

The probation wards at Halfway Street and Burnt Oak Lane entrances could admit 40 children at a time. The first 109 children were admitted on 22 September 1902. By the end of the month there were 422 children in Sidcup Homes. The following year there were 558. Some were unsuitable. In October, Nellie Norman and three other girls were discharged to Witham Ringworm Hospital. Four were returned to Greenwich Workhouse at Grove Park. Frequently parents took the children back, presumably now being able to care for them.

From the 26 admissions on 17 February 1904, eight had a parent with an address (this includes two who had an aunt); 11 had parents in the workhouse, two were registered as 'out of House' presumably meaning just discharged but unable to look after the children; four had parents in prison and the mother of one was in an infirmary.

At the other end, strenuous efforts were made to find placements for children. Sometimes the records read as if the Homes were factories for producing disciplined workers. Probably neither the Guardians nor the senior staff would have considered this in any way remiss. They wanted to produce young people who could look after themselves, lead moral lives, and not end up in the workhouse as so many of their parents did.

The first and most difficult hurdle was finding children a 'situation' at 14 or 15. The great problem was that it was impossible for a job to be found which carried sufficient wages for these young people to live on. 'Therefore the only means of disposing of them is by obtaining situations where bed and board are found, or indoor apprenticeship', the Headmaster wrote in 1906. The best type of placement was when a boy could be sent to work as an apprentice and given bed and board plus a sum of money while he learned a trade, which would keep him for the rest of his life.

Not all offers of work were accepted. The Headmaster refused an application for a boy worker from a hairdresser in New Cross Road because 'I think we should do better for our boys than this'. Presumably this hairdresser was not offering an apprenticeship but just wanted a cheap worker. Similarly, the Guardians refused to allow a chimney sweep to come and select a boy to work with him.

Moving children on was always welcome if it was to a future where they would be under adequate supervision, so it was satisfactory when five boys aged 11–13 'expressed a desire to go to Exmouth [where there was a training ship] to be trained for the navy'. The District Messengers Company asked for three boys who would live at St. Andrew's Home, Westminster, and were kitted out by the Guardians with a suit and boots.

Some placements were unsuccessful. William G. was returned from his position as a page for a lady in Hampstead, 'As he has apparently some growth in his nose which is not very desirable in a page'. She was therefore permitted to come and select a boy more to her taste, one George Jenkinson. Another boy was 'removed from his situation on account of wet habits. It is hoped he will overcome this.'

To give an idea of the numbers: during 1906, 25 boys over 14 years of age were discharged to work situations and 7 boys over 13 were discharged to relatives. In 1907, 33 were placed 'in situations'. Joseph Steer kept in contact with the boys to ensure the placement was successful, something on which he reported regularly to the School Homes Committee.

Girls were put 'in service': that is, were trained as servants. Of 34 girls over the age of 14 reported on in November 1906 five were already selected for service; in three cases negotiations were pending; 11 were mentally or physically unfit for service; 11 needed further training; and four were emigrating to Canada.

Barnardo's Homes had a scheme for organising 'the immigration of pauper children into Canada'. For £9 sponsorship money per child the Greenwich Guardians could send some of theirs. The School Homes Committee stated, 'We feel it would be advantageous to send boys to Canada under the scheme, and ask the authority of the Board (of Guardians) to make all the preliminary arrangements with a view to the early emigration of any boys who may be suitable'. There was no mention here of consulting the boys but in a later reference boys did 'express their willingness' to emigrate.

One member of the Board of Guardians proposed in 1904 to send

100 children from Sidcup to Canada – presumably the children would have little choice in this and it was just a way of getting the numbers down. Just setting a quota for compulsory emigration like this was obviously seen as impractical and it was not pursued, but clearly it had the effect of stimulating the emigration programme as in 1906, 33 children were earmarked to go. It is unlikely that such numbers could have been achieved without compulsion. It must have been a miserable time for these children, who would have to leave what family they had and go to a completely unknown country. South Africa was also looking for emigrants though nothing like so actively as Canada.

Other organisations might help find 'situations': the Association for Befriending Boys, or the Metropolitan Association for Befriending Young Servants (MABYS) for girls. The Headmaster lamented in 1909 that there were about 12 children, 'who are below the average intellectually'. He suggested they should be sent to the Metropolitan Asylums Board training school for feeble-minded children. On another occasion he wrote, 'I am bringing four crippled boys before the Guardians. I find it impossible to place these boys.' Such children were generally dispatched to a cripples' home.

The Guardians would attempt to 'move on' anyone who did not fit. They tried to have the Metropolitan Asylums Board take an epileptic boy, William Shirley, but that Board replied that the only places for epileptics they had were in 'Imbecile Asylums' and as he was not an imbecile there was no accommodation for him.

The School Homes Committee minutes reported that 'Harriet Bray was again giving trouble. The committee gave instructions for measures to be taken for her admission to a Metropolitan Asylums Board Home for Defective Children' but they refused to accept her (perhaps because she was not 'defective', but just disobedient) so an application was made to the Metropolitan Association for Befriending Young Servants. This leads to a question of exactly what sort of homes this organisation ran, if a placement with them was considered to be appropriate for a difficult child. Similarly, in 1905 the Head Mistress reported that Gladys Brennan continued to give great trouble, and instructions were given for her to be sent to a MABYS home.

The people making decisions about the future of children in the homes sometimes showed a disappointing lack of professionalism.

The *Kentish Mercury* reported on 24 August 1906 on an open meeting of the Special Committee on the accommodation of children, which was discussing a widow who had two children at Sidcup. She was in the habit of taking them away for one or two days then brought them back, often late at night. The discussion of whether the children should be taken from her by the Guardians descended into silly jocularities and sexual innuendo: 'Mr Abbott said the woman had three children and there would be more. The Chairman knew her well (loud laughter). She was a dark woman (more laughter). Mr Oldman: I don't see the joke. The Chairman: This is not a laughing matter. It is most serious. Mr Abbott: It is. He admitted he was thinking of the woman (more laughter) – her conduct he meant. The Chairman: I am thinking of the little ones'.

Before the First World War

In 1906, although Sidcup Homes had been in existence for only a few years the Old Boys had an annual meeting at the Homes on Whit Mondays. A representative of the *Kentish Mercury* asked Headmaster Mr Steer whether, as the result of being brought up in such rural surroundings the boys were led to a love for life and work in the country, or whether the town had a greater fascination in regard to their future. The answer the headmaster gave was said to be the 'pleasing information' that about 44 boys who attended, 'there were half a dozen who were absent and the number who have left the Homes since they opened is 60, but six are soldiers, one or two are dead, and some are far away from London. Only one had been sent back to the Greenwich Workhouse and most follow the occupation of gardeners, so that the Sidcup Homes are playing part in the great problem of over population of the big city and lack of tillers of the soil'. That same year the children's Homes Committee reported that Henry Matthews, aged 15, one of the boys at Sidcup Homes, had won a London County Council Junior Scholarship in gardening, including free tuition at the Royal Botanic Society's Gardens and a grant of £20 per annum.

The Guardians sent round inspectors to maintain standards. An inspector stopped the milk cart from the Yeldham Dairy Company delivering to the homes one day in 1906 and tested the milk. One of the churns was found to have been watered down so the Guardians prosecuted the supplier but the dairyman had given a false name to the inspector. The summons was therefore made out in the wrong name and the court dismissed the case as reported on 21 August 1906. No doubt the Guardians cancelled the contract. In 1907 and 1908 the homes cost around eleven and a half thousand pounds a year to run.

There was a fire at The Hollies Mansion in May 1907 when the whole of the roof of the old building and the upper staircase was destroyed. Sidcup and Foots Cray Fire Brigade turned out, for which they charged £14.3s. (£14.15p). The cause of the fire was faulty construction: there were wooden beams under the fireplace that ignited.

From 1909 Joseph Steer was appointed head of the whole establishment, the steward's post being abolished. The steward had earlier been censured for permitting 'abstraction and misappropriation of stores'. Specifically, a sack of potatoes had gone missing from the stores and had been found in the engineer's room; and cleaning fluid had been thrown away – the object being to buy more and make commission on the purchase. Clearly the Board of Guardians felt this was a small token of a larger fraud. The steward and his wife were given £262 in compensation for being made redundant. This was two and a half years' salary.

Efforts were made to remove children from the pernicious influence of parents, but some proposals went too far. The Guardians of Newcastle wrote in 1911 that they were 'desirous of exchanging children at present in their Homes whose parents or relatives are likely to exercise an evil influence over their after-life for an equal number of similar children from Unions in different parts of the country', and asking whether the Guardians were prepared to consider such an exchange. The reply was terse: 'in our opinion the difficulties are very great and the advantages small. We do not therefore consider it desirable to make such arrangements'.

The children at Sidcup Homes were invited to participate in the celebrations for the Coronation of George V in 1911 by the Sidcup Coronation Committee. As reported in the *Kentish Mercury* on 2 June 1911, the committee was raising a fund to entertain all the children of the neighbourhood for half a day in Foots Cray Park. Every child would be presented with a flag and a coronation mug, tea would be provided and there would be organised sports and a display of fireworks. The Guardians contributed £20 and agreed unanimously that 500 children from the Homes would take part while children

The fire at The Hollies Mansion, May 1907.

who were too small to do so would have treats for tea.

In January 1911, the children's committee reported that the Kent Educational Committee had asked whether the swimming baths at Sidcup Homes might be used by children from outside elementary schools, and if so, upon what terms and conditions. It was decided to reply 'that such use of the bath could not be allowed'.

People who had no direct contact with the Homes were concerned about standards. When a rumour circulated that the Guardians had denied children bacon and eggs to save money, the radical Member of Parliament for Huddersfield, A. Sherwell, asked the President of the Local Government Board about it. The minister contacted the Guardians and, as reported in the *Kentish Mercury* on 19 March 1915, he had to explain in the House of Commons that 'the supply of eggs and bacon was discontinued for a time owing to the high prices of these articles, but it was resumed when the prices dropped to a reasonable figure'.

3

The First World War
and the 20s

On 6 August 1914, when the First World War had just begun, it was recorded that two male members of staff had been called up; one was in the Territorials and the other in the Reserves. The following month the Headmaster's book finishes and there are no further ones in the archives. In June 1914 there were 221 boys and 311 girls and infants in the homes, a total of 532. In November 1915 Lamorbey School (the day elementary school) was forced to close because of bombing.

A former pupil, Victor Froude, a Sergeant in the Lancashire Fusiliers, was awarded the Military Medal and Distinguished Conduct Medal during the war. The *Kentish Mercury* on 17 November 1916, under the heading 'Sidcup boy's gallantry', printed Victor C. Froude's letter thanking the Guardians for the congratulations he received on being awarded decorations for bravery on the field of battle. He wrote: 'I think I am one of the first Sidcup boys to win a decoration, and I am proud to wear it, not because I myself have gained the distinction, but because of the great honour and credit which is reflected on my old school at Sidcup, and on the Guardians, foster-parents and teachers of that grand and splendid institution. From the bottom of my heart I sincerely hope that I may be the first of many, many more to bring such glory to dear old Sidcup'. The same newspaper reported later in the month that Lance Corporal Arthur Lloyd and Sergeant L. E. Redman, London Regiment, other old boys of Sidcup Homes, were also awarded the Military Medal.

The Greenwich Grove Park Workhouse was occupied by the military, and other institutions, like Sidcup, were under greater pressure. There were 705 children in 1917, 618 in 1918. Staff were increasingly 'called to colours' and soon every man of military age had either been signed up or rejected. The self-sufficiency of which Sidcup had always been proud increased in the war. In 1918, the Homes made 4,827 items of clothing. During the First World War 40 boys from the Homes were killed. One of them, Cecil Cornell, was particularly unlucky, being killed the day before the armistice. The schoolkeeper, Mr Small, was killed in 1916.

In May 1920, Mr Steer in a conclusion speech at the 'old boys' reunion gathering said the homes were once again in full working order. The boys were at the top of the Greenwich Schools Cricket League. In more sombre mood, the *Kentish Mercury* under the subheading: 'War Memorial Unveiled', described the unveiling of the Homes' war memorial in May 1921. 'A large number of members of the Greenwich Union Board of Guardians and friends at the Guardians' children's home at Sidcup attended on Whit Monday for the occasion of the wooden panel which had been placed in the gymnasium to commemorate 40 "old boys" who made the supreme sacrifice in the War'.

'Of the 212 who joined before conscription, 37 were killed on the field of battle, two have died since, and 12 have gained honours. The 'old boys' have defrayed the cost of the panel, which is a beautiful piece of work . . . The children, to the number of 800, also attended, together with several of their foster parents'.

Mr F. J. Oldman, representing the Homes Committee, said 'they owed to those whose names it bore the highest tribute it was possible to pay', unveiled the panel, covered with the Union Jack, and they would always honour their memory. Mr Steer then read the names on the panel, at the top of which is the inscription:

> To the glory of God, and in memory of the old boys
> who fell in the Great War
> 1914–1918.

The names are as follows:

> R. Arnold, E. Allchurch, R. Arnett, H. Bake, H. Belton,
> C. Benfield and S. Benfield (brothers),
> H. Bowie, Brewer and R. Brewer (brothers),
> T. Bryant, E. Burns, F. Cornell, W. Fellowas,
> W. Holding and P. Holding (brothers),
> W. Hunt, W. Kirk, G. Lloyd, C. Litson,

T. Mallett, J. Miller, G. Morris,

J. Puplett and S. Puplett (brothers), J. Salter, G. Smears,

H. Self and H. Self (brothers), J. Smith and T. Smith (brothers),

C. Upton and E. Upton (brothers)

G. Ward, C. Watling, J. White and G. White (brothers),

P. Willis, J. Wright and J. Wrightson.

The memorial was dedicated by Mr Challenor and Mr Bonner (bandmaster) sounded the 'Last Post' and 'Reveille.' Mr Davis was at the harmonium, and the band accompanied the singing. Then Wreaths were placed at the foot of the memorial by Mr Steer, the 'old boys,' the officers, and the children. After luncheon a cricket match was played between Beeches and Firs, and Limes and Oaks, the latter winning by 54 runs to 50.

The 1920s

In the first years of the twentieth century children were set to work scrubbing the floors of the Homes before they went to school. A Mrs Amos who sat on the Board of Guardians brought the matter to a head with a motion 'that no child of school age shall be allowed to scrub or polish floors in any of the guardians' institutions'. Mrs Cunis, who had only recently joined the Board, was supportive and said it was obvious that children had been involved in scrubbing since the homes were opened and she was shocked that in this civilised age there were 'slave children'. The vote over the matter resulted in a stalemate, however, as reported in the *Kentish Mercury* of 6 July 1923, with seven voting on each side, so the policy was not changed but it was clearly being challenged.

The Guardians liked to maintain contact with parents from whom they could expect a contribution to their funds. Lydia Myles, for example, was working as a servant at 17s.6d. (87p) a week less 2s.6d. (12p) for washing. She had a 14-year-old boy at Sidcup, 'the child of a bigamous marriage' for whom she was offering the Guardians 3s.6d. (17p) a week. The Accommodation Committee remarked on 18 September 1923, 'We recommend she be called upon to pay 5s.0d. (25p) weekly towards the cost of her child's maintenance.'

In September 1923 there were 577 children at the Lamorbey Residential School, formerly the Sidcup Homes. In 1924, parents were vetoed to see if they could have their children home for the summer holidays, and 26 applications were considered.

To some extent, the Homes operated as a cheap childminding service for the desperately poor or simply for single parents whose work took them away from home. On 5 May 1925 there was an application by Henry Long – to have his child Eugene, aged five, admitted to Shirley Schools. He was already paying 2s.6d. (12.5p) weekly for William, a child he already had there. From 1925 to 1930 the Homes were called Greenwich and Deptford Children's Homes.

In 1925 there was a fire at The Limes in the early hours of 30 May. All 52 boys were downstairs and out of the building within two minutes and there was no injury.

On Fair Day, the school magazine recorded, 'once a year the Guardians provided swings, a roundabout, donkeys, coconut shies etc. and gave the children a treat in the school meadow'. The children were given discs valued from 9d. to 1s.6d. (4p to 7.5p) depending on their age which they could spend as they liked. The band played at the Den, Millwall's football ground, at home games on Saturday afternoons.

The Greenwich and Deptford Guardians' different opinions on expenditure at Sidcup were reflected in public debate. A letter to the Editor of the *Kentish Mercury* appeared in the paper in 1928:

'Sir, – I understand the Greenwich Board of Guardians have just appointed, or are about to appoint, a female swimming instructress to teach the girls to swim, as they do not think it right or proper for a mere man to teach children of the opposite sex. I suppose they have never heard of mixed bathing. At any rate they seem ignorant, or innocent, of the fact that England is a Bankrupt nation, and that is their business to stop creating new posts for new officials – they had better follow the example of the LCC and take steps to curtail their expenditure and reduce their expensive staff wherever necessary. When 1 was young no one outside Bedlam would have dared to suggest wasting the ratepayers' money on teaching youngsters to swim – if we wanted to learn we had to teach ourselves in the nearest canal, stream or pond. Why should poor little nervous children who hate the water be compelled to go and learn to swim, at the ratepayers' expense too, or else be chided by their fellow schoolmates for not going?

I also hear the same Board are about to appoint two more teachers – why not reduce the hours of teaching, instead of adding to the expense? A few hours less cramming a week would not hurt the poor children. No wonder poor mites are tired out when they come home – too tired to get up in the morning. If they would teach the children a few things, such as reading, writing and arithmetic, and manners, properly, and many poor little, ones would have a far happier childhood than they do at present.

– I am, Sir, etc., A.E.S.'

Such criticisms had their effect. At a meeting of the Greenwich Guardians, in October 1929, it was revealed by the chairman of the visiting committee that to date the sum of £15 had been raised to buy the children's 'wireless set'. This clearly displeased the Guardians and rather than provide the children with the wireless the money was refunded to the donors.

Workhouses and the working of the Poor Law continued to be criticised into the 1920s, with such politicians as William Mosses, a member of the Greenwich Board of Guardians, criticising the award of money to 'able-bodied young fellows who came for relief week after week with the same story that they could not find work'.

In the Summer of 1927 a resolution by the Greenwich Guardians to buy a set of new uniforms for the boys of Sidcup Children's Home band was considered. The present uniforms were described as 'green and ripe with age' and some of them were in deplorable condition. Nevertheless, Mr W. Mosses regarded the proposed expenditure as a 'waste of money' and after the inevitable wrangling he carried the day and the resolution was defeated.

Speaking to the South East and Kidbrooke Conservative Association, Mr Mosses criticised the Sidcup Homes. He said the children cost £2 a week each to keep, while 'most working mothers had to bring up their children at much less per head than that, and he was sorry to observe some of the children brought up at the Sidcup Homes coming back to the relief stations for relief . . . they were not taught the self-reliance and adventurous spirit that was necessary to earn a living these days. While not deprecating sport, he felt more time might be spent on education; in short, he thought the whole system of educa-tion and administration at the Sidcup Homes was wrong'.

Mr Mosses, a magistrate who had been awarded the OBE for his public work, was clearly on a crusade. He addressed the Charlton Women Conservatives in March 1928 to tell them the children at Sidcup were 'much better looked after than the children of ratepay-ers in Greenwich and Deptford. One would have thought that in these circumstances they would raise a race of super men and women, but last Thursday he had interviewed three Sidcup boys who had applied for relief. It was very regrettable that these boys, who, after training, had been placed in situations, and had failed to keep and came back to the source from which they sprang – the work-house (where they were now) – complaining that circumstances were too much for them'. Mr Mosses complained that they paid school-teachers on the same scale that was used for teachers in ordinary schools, 'yet they never heard of any of the boys graduating to cen-tral and continuation schools'.

Mr Mosses was not unopposed, however. At the next meeting of the Board of Guardians, as reported in the *Kentish Mercury* on 23 March 1928, the Board distanced themselves from his remarks. They did, however, ask for the head teacher to report to them every month on the education of children at Sidcup so they clearly thought that Mosses had a case. The headmaster, the newly-appointed F.W. Ockenden, told the governors 'that the children have a far better edu-cation than children of the same class outside . . . We have six boys attending Greenwich Central School and two more are to start after Easter. Three girls attend a Central School and two who left last year have both gained admission to Central Schools, obviously on the education they get here'.

The assertive Mr Mosses declared his objective had been met with the Guardians calling for monthly reports on education at the schools. He protested, 'We take more interest in the Sidcup pigs than we do in the Sidcup boys and we are more often seen around the Sidcup styes than we are around the Sidcup schoolrooms'.

Another board member, Mrs Cunis, declared that Mosses was 'absolutely warped and biased', and she had looked into education when she first came on to the Board six years previously. The result of visits she made then was the introduction of continuation train-ing in tailoring, shoe-making, plumbing, carpentry and gardening.

The girls were destined to become servants but some girls, she said, were 'bright and fluffy' and more suited to shop work than domestic service. She called them 'fluffy, pale, pink little girls' and defended an alternative career choice for them, saying, 'all women are not domestic servants and all wives are not drudges'. Four girls from the Homes gained employment in the Royal households and many titled families. 'So it shows that we do get our girls into decent situations', she said.

At a committee meeting of the Greenwich Guardians on 7 March 1929, Mr Mosses, JP, objected 'to the way individual Guardians are fathering the grievances of our employees'. He said that there was hardly a meeting of the Board at which Mr Bright did not press the claims of some disgruntled person. Mr Bright seemed to be receptacle of all the discontent of the staff both in Greenwich and at Sidcup. 'They never come to me', he added, amidst laughter from board members. Employees, he contended, had a proper way of ventilating their grievances, and that was through the superior officers. Mr Bright said nobody could ever accuse him of dishonesty or deceit. The man in point came to him with his grievance and said, 'You are a trade unionist'? He said, 'Yes', and Mr Bright replied, 'Why not ask your trade union to write to the Board?'

In November 1928 there were 440 children living there. Many of the staff were at the Homes a very long time. Mrs Haws, who had been housemother at the Oaks for 20 years, died in 1928. Nurse Campion died after 23 years work in 1925. The staff numbered 159 in 1929, of whom 60 were resident.

In April 1928 a recommendation was tabled by the Sidcup House Committee that a shotgun be purchased for the Superintendent to shoot crows which were destroying the crops at the rate of 1000 cabbages a year. This gave rise to a hilarious debate in which it was pointed out that the proposal made no provision for ammunition and that the Superintendent would not be empowered to shoot rabbits, sparrows, pigeons or other ground vermin. In any event, however many crows he slaughtered there would always be others to take their place, and of course there was always the attendant danger of injury to the boys and any passers-by who had the misfortune to cross the Superintendent's field of fire.

A Mrs Vincent suggested that if certain members of the committee turned up at the farm it would be more than sufficient to scare all the crows away. In the end it was decided to delete the proposal from the agenda by 11 votes to 5.

The Homes had an association with Howard House, a hostel for boys in Hampstead. Its warden was able to say how all of the boys were doing. Many were at Smithfield Market School for butchers; there were two tailors; one had emigrated and was now a sheep farmer; one was doing hotel work; one was a footman 'at a society lady's in Kensington'; one was ill in hospital and one was 'lost sight of'.

The Band was still going strong. Many former bandsmen joined the forces. There was Band-Sergeant Wilkins of 2nd Battalion, the Rifle Brigade. Walter Trevitt of the Border Regiment was at Kneller Hall (Royal Military School of Music), a pupil on cornet and violin. Two were in the Wiltshire Regiment (cornet and clarinet). Sam Wheeler had left the services and was playing trombone at the New Cross Empire. There were two in the City Police.

Trades taught at the Homes included tailoring, shoe repairs, plumbing, baking and carpentry. Some jobs that old boys went into were compositor, joiner, stock exchange worker, steward on liner, clerk at sports club, building trade, confectioner, metal worker, shop fitter, jewellery trade, gym instructor, dairy worker, tailoring, hotel work, footman, butcher and baker; some had emigrated to Australia.

The Annual Sports Day during the summer of 1929 attracted 1,200 visitors, who marched past the entire Home, led by the band.

Metropolitan Association for Befriending Young Servants

Girls who were problematic were put under the care of the Metropolitan Association for Befriending Young Servants. MABYS also visited girls who had been placed in service at least once in their first year to check on their progress. The mistress of the house where they were in service was asked to be helpful to the MABYS visitor but clearly she was the servant's 'friend', not that of the mistress, and there is an implication that these visitors were regarded as interfering busybodies.

The Schools Committee asked for a report on the girls under MABYS training, which was received in January 1930. The following are details from three of them:

'Mary H., 19, at Sidcup 1916-27.
Both parents are of an illiterate type and whole history of long

chargeability is sordid and without redeeming features.

February 1928: Nothing in girl's mental condition to account for failure in work and energy.

September 1928: Gives no trouble. Very bad worker. Mentally dull and stupid. Doubtful if she will ever do any good.

January 1928: Tries, but incapable. Mother always writing letters wanting her home. Letters withheld. Not ready for service.

December 1928: Tries hard but is really incapable and dull. Cannot recommend service.

September 1929: Improved. Willing and helpful. Not often rude. Not a good worker. Slack at times. Keen to learn and interested in cooking. Needs training in work and character'.

'Dorothy at Sidcup 1920-25 went to Denmark Hill Hostel.

Home conditions very poor. Girl is a cripple (T.B. Hip – infantile paralysis).

29 July 1927: complaints received regarding her conduct that she was very amorous and a young man was cautioned. She was sent to MABYS, placed in service but left. Worked with a firm in Margaret Street but reported to be difficult and unsteady. Returned to MABYS and on 28 February 1929 girl stated her intention, "Not to be under anyone's supervision – did not intend to go straight and would please herself" and left hostel to go to parents. Brought back by General Relieving Officer 21 February 1929 placed at Sister Mabel Club, Drury Lane. Started work 26 August 1929 at Salvation Army Trade Department 12s.0d. (60p).

December 1929: health good, conduct good. Quite happy in present work and superintendent gives her a good character'.

'Alice K., 16, at Sidcup 1925-8.

Both parents living apart, co-habiting and have illegitimate children. In consequence of home conditions, child was adopted.

June 1929: Conduct not good. Very lazy and independent. Very difficult girl to deal with.

September 1929: Independent, dirty and lazy. Shows no improvement or progress.

December 1929: Rude, dirty, thoroughly indifferent to all work. May be a little weak mentally.

This girl's mother has, on several occasions, endeavoured to entice girl away from her situation, but in February last was severely warned since when no definite complaints have been received'.

MABYS thus seems to have acted as a moral police force, keeping a control over girls until well into maturity. Presumably such control could be exercised until the girls reached 21 which was legal adulthood.

The Children's Homes Committee officers would use the services of MABYS to deal with what he saw were urgent cases. On 27 July 1922 the committee minutes note: 'We have received an unsatisfactory report regarding the conduct of Mabel F. who was discharged to service some time ago. Prompt action has been taken by MABYS at the request of the clerk with a view to saving the girl from ruin. The Association asks that if necessary the girl may be sent to a Rescue Home at approximate cost of 10s.0d. (50p) a week.'

There was some discussion of what to do with girls who were suffering from various physical and mental defects 'until arrangement were made for them to be put in a "MABYS certified home for suitable cases"'.

A report of January 1934 on the previous year gave the girls' view of MABYS, 'It hasn't been necessary to send any girls to the Mabys training homes. We understand that there is a strong feeling amongst girls that that to have to be sent to one of these homes is something to be avoided if possible'.

MABYS notified the London County Council in 1943 of its intention to discontinue its activities. The LCC assumed its responsibilities, taking over the Association's hostel at 94 Oakley Street sw3, known after 1945 as Mavis Hostel.

4

The 1930s

In 1929 the Homes were certified for 570 children. There were places for 247 boys and 323 girls. Further accommodation was provided for 26 boys and girls in the isolation infirmary block. The annual sports day in 1929 was attended by 1,200 visitors, and the event began with the entire Home marching past the school led by the band.

In 1930 the London County Council took over the establishment which at that time was called Sidcup Residential School. In July 1930 it was re-named Lamorbey Residential School (the Home was not called The Hollies until 1950, though, somewhat confusingly, there had always been a single building on the site called The Hollies).

In a survey of 1931 the school is shown to cover 65 acres of which three and a half are ornamental gardens, 11 playing fields and 40 under cultivation – the farm. The fields around the Homes, that previously had been used for horse ploughing, gradually disappeared to

The Band: many of whom entered military bands on leaving the Home.

41

Gardening remained an important activity.

be over taken by new roads and housing. The outside world was gradually beginning to close in on the Homes' boundaries.

Perhaps in an attempt to humanise the site, linoleum covered the floors over the ground floor of each house and upstairs the floor was polished. Curtains and pictures were provided for the first time. Scrubbing, the bane of earlier days, was now reduced to a minimum. Stainless steel knives were replacing the old steel ones.

The administration area comprised: the Superintendent's quarters, office, committee room, staff dining room, meat store, general store, kitchen and maids' quarters. The central block was the gymnasium (also used for religious services), swimming bath, laundry, engineer's shop, plumber's shop, bakery and boiler house. The workshop block had the painter's shop, carpenter's shop, bootmaker's shop, tailor's shop, needle room, band room and mess room.

An inspector's report of November 1931 said, the school 'was dull, lifeless, and badly organised. Schemes of work and methods of instruction were old fashioned and the equipment was inadequate; and the day school carried on its work with practically no contact whatsoever with the life of the children out of school hours. In the comparatively short time he has been at the school the Headmaster in charge has worked extremely hard to modernise the teaching, the scheme of work and the equipment'.

It was felt desirable 'to secure for deserving boys and girls a more advanced or specialised form of education'. The Headmaster looked for promising pupils to encourage and in the five years to 1935 Lamorbey was the only one of the residential schools from which a pupil gained a Junior County Scholarship. However, the Headmaster had to acknowledge in a report in October 1932, 'The general intelligence of the children is probably below average for London elementary school children.'

There were typical bureaucratic problems with the changeover to the LCC. Because of the council's regional banding system, staff were now paid at a different (and lower) grade from that which had been the case under the Guardians. In 1935 it was reported that six of the most able teachers had left since the school was transferred to the LCC. This loss of good staff and the difficulty in appointing people, who could earn more in a neighbouring school, led to an inspector's report of January 1935. 'The staff, taken as a whole, is below average in teaching ability and in power of control, before the advent of the present Headmaster a repressive type of discipline was used. The

Joan Richmond, aged 13, netball captain and school prefect, holding the ball for the blues – Sir Philip Sidney team. (See her 'Account' on page 116).

43

school was quiet, it was also dull and intellectually almost dead . . .
on the other hand, changes towards a freer discipline appear to have
been too rapid, both for the children and the staff'.

In September 1936 the day school was transferred to Kent
Education Committee as a junior school. Arrangements were made
for children in the locality to attend the school as well as children
who lived in the Homes. Children in the Homes attended local
elementary schools.

The managing committee required reports on sex instruction and
the Superintendent obliged with this report, on 22 October 1936:
'During the past year there has been almost an entire absence of any
matters in which sex played an important part'. On 25 November 1937
the similar report came: 'During the year it has not been necessary
for any special attention to be drawn to sex matters and the Matron
and the Superintendent have continued to give suitable instruction
to individual children when necessary. The Chaplain, when preparing the children for Confirmation, also avails himself of the opportunity to give some instruction to the boys on sex matters'. Girls
were, presumably, considered asexual until marriage.

The *Kentish Mercury* in January 1930 reported that a proposal to
award pocket money to the children was opposed by the Ministry.
They said there was 'no legal authority for the indiscriminate award
of pocket money to children chargeable to the Poor Law Authorities'
though prizes for good conduct could be awarded. In order to get
round the ban, the Guardians decided to award all the children prizes
for good conduct, in accordance with the scale they had already
adopted for money. Children of ten would get a penny a week; 10 to
12, two pence; and over that, three pence a week. A tuck shop was to
be built for children to spend their money.

When the LCC took over, the managing committee declared all
children should have an annual holiday. In 1932, 250 children aged
5–12 went to the zoo and had tea, and 200 older children went to
Margate and Ramsgate and had tea. For two weeks in 1933, 550 children went to Dymchurch. Later the children over 10 were to go to
Walton-on-the-Naze. It was joked that when they entered the sea all
together the tide came in another six inches!

Older children later started going on journeys with the schools
they attended. Some children went on visits to foreign countries
with the World Friendship Association. In an unusual item – perhaps

unique in this series of records – there is a page written by a child in the file. In it Annie Day explains, 'The aim of the World Friendship Association is shown in its name. It is to enable us to understand and to make friends with people of other countries'.

Friendless Children

There was great concern for 'friendless children' in the 1930s, as there had not been in the previous decades. It was suggested by the managing committee, 'that a suitable letter to one of the leading newspapers or a wireless appeal might result in some to response from people living in the neighbourhood of the school'.

A conference on friendless children was held, probably in early 1934, for all chairs and vice chairs of managing committees of homes and all LCC Special Services Sub-Committee members, and it was agreed that little had been done for this class of children, and action was necessary. The number at Lamorbey Residential School was estimated to be 60 but the estimate was later considered to be excessive.

It was agreed that 'all friendless children considered as suitable should if possible be Boarded Out', that is, fostered. It was estimated in October 1934 that there were 24 children without friends, or worthy friends, outside the school. Local residents had been found to take an interest in some of them. The report remarked, 'It will be realised that any scheme whereby local residents are allowed to have even the temporary care of our children must be carefully watched, and the Superintendent is alive to the difficulty'.

Work on Discharge

In a 1936 report of boys found places since the last meeting: 9 were messenger and shop boys; 2 went into shoemaking; 3 became page boys; 2 went into a bakery; 2 became kitchen boys; 2 office boys; 5 in metal work; 1 was apprenticed (though to whom is not recorded); 8 went to the Training Ship Exmouth; and 16 into Army bands. Of all the boys who left LCC care in the year ended September 1935, the most common occupations were: 79 in hotels and pottering; 53 in army bands; 69 in engineering and mechanical work; 50 in shop delivery work. For this last category boys were expected to ride bicycles, so the managing committee bought one for boys to practise on.

Domestic service was still the lot of most girls; they received £18 a

Girls in Lamorbey School playground, summer 1931.

year for work as a 'kitchen maid', 'under housemaid' or 'between maid'.

The Fairbridge Farm School in Western Australia still took many children via the Child Emigration Society but there must have been bad reports circulating about these placements because in April 1932 the managing committee decided not to send any more children there and reaffirmed this in 1933. Some improvement must have taken place by 1935, as there was agreement for four girls to go to another Fairbridge Farm School, Vancouver Island, British Columbia.

Wireless sets were bought for all the cottages in 1934 and a cinematography projector for the school. In the mid 1930s, indoor activities at the homes included gymnastics, billiards, table tennis, badminton, darts, ring nets, dominoes, playing cards, chess, draughts, snakes and ladders, etc. There was a reading and writing room, dancing and singing classes and scripture classes.

There must have been some boxing arranged at the school, or with an outside club, as one boy who was entered for the Kent County Boxing League won the final bout in his class in 1936.

Jewish Children

When the leases were due to run out on the houses which formed the Stepney Jewish Children's Home, Lamorbey's managing body was asked if they could make over some space for the children. They replied in November 1934, 'We are glad to inform the subcommittee that we concur in the proposal to accommodate these children in three cottages at Lamorbey Residential School and to cordially invite Jewish representation on our managing committee.' Six Jewish members were later appointed.

Cottages were made welcoming for the Jewish children: the right hand door posts were given a Mezuzah (a small piece of parchment containing a scriptural verse as commanded in Deuteronomy vi 9) and kitchen areas were made ready to accommodate some (or perhaps all) orthodox Jewish dietary requirements. The managing committee and staff were given information sheets on Jewish religious custom, for example the Tallis (praying shawls) and Bar-Mitzvah for boys at 13; the necessity of keeping Sabbath and Passover.

There was an even faster turnover of Jewish children than of the usual clients of the homes and numbers increased from the anticipated 60 to 100, when it was necessary to open a fourth cottage. It is agreeable to think of the hospitality being extended to Jewish children when such cruelty was taking place in Germany, but accommodating them was not without its problems. A report on 22 May 1936 noted, 'There seemed to be a feeling among the older pupils that there was some danger of "their school" being overrun by Jewish children'. In 1937 there were 100 Jewish children out of 420.

It was difficult for the managing committee to find a Jewish housemother and father – a father being particularly important because of the importance of a male figure in Jewish family ritual. Eventually the Head Office of the United Synagogue found a young man, Mr Richardson, who was being trained for the ministry, and who was prepared to visit to officiate on the Sabbath, which meant staying at the homes from sunset on Friday until sunset on Saturday each week.

This was only a short-term solution and the problems persisted. In 1946 the Jewish children were spread around, the girls in Myrtle and the boys in Oaks and Beeches. There were still discussions that 'a cottage with a Jewish staff be made available so that service, festivals and feasts be properly observed and the food problem solved.' M. Zeffertt, a Jewish chaplain, visited regularly and reported to the management committee.

By the late 1940s, it was suggested the Jewish children could all go to the Jewish Orphanage, so their religious requirements could be met more easily. But the orphanage did not wish to take all the Jewish children – wanting only girls under 12 and, in general, children with no apparent problems. It was decided to offer the Jewish Orphanage the opportunity of seeing Jewish children from the 'receiving home' at Lamorbey. Those Jewish children who remained in the council's care would be treated the same as the other children 'except that the Jewish authorities would be told of them and invited to make appropriate arrangements for their religious upbringing'.

When the bulk of the Jewish children left, the Superintendent wrote he was sorry to see them go, 'The Jewish girls are a pattern as regards behaviour and industry and the boys are fairly amenable'.

5

The Second World War
and After

Lamorbey Residential School was used as an evacuation centre for boys compulsorily evacuated from London – presumably those who did not go voluntarily on the government's orders.

There was bombing, though nothing like so severe as the bombing of London. Still, as the Superintendent wrote in November 1943, 'For many months in succession the children have had to be taken from their beds and taken refuge in the strong room [the best built room in the house?], so the staff have had an anxious time. Fortunately no physical injuries have been suffered'.

There were discussions on the erection of blast walls to protect the buildings, or bricking up the windows to a height of seven feet to create a secure ground floor in which children and staff could sleep. At one time 97 windows were damaged, some for the second time, and parts of ceilings collapsed due to the blast of a bomb nearby. Bombings did little lasting damage to the buildings excepting to one double cottage that had to be rebuilt.

After World War II, there was a more relaxed atmosphere about the school, with small groups of children often being seen in Woolworth's or around Sidcup High Street on Saturday afternoons. This was part of a concentrated effort to improve standards of child care and education at the school. In 1937 the Head of Homes produced a blueprint for the future of Lamorbey Residential School, a proposed five-year plan for improvements. The war inevitably delayed full implementation but changes which were eventually seen in the 1940s were in line with these aims: 'To concentrate on the welfare of the "Deprived Child" and to give (him) every opportunity of attaining an all round, moral, physical and mental development – a cultural background to foster round and independent judgement, a satisfactory standard of poise, elegance and tone, so as not to become only a good responsible citizen but acquire and exhibit a sense of beauty and creative ability'. 'All projects and efforts should be directed to attain this end and all consideration of staffing, equipment and environment, should as far as humanly possible, be subservient to fostering and attaining this desired condition'.

As part of the plan to bring poor law children into contact with the Outside World, the internal school was given up and the children attended several Kent schools. All the infants attended the Halfway Street School (in the former Lamorbey School premises), the juniors except for two or three went to Burnt Oak Lane Junior mixed school. The seniors went to Blackfen and Sidcup Central schools where there were separate departments for girls and boys.

On the future of girls after leaving the Homes the report commented, 'In the past school leavers have mostly been trained for domestic service and most of the training has been given within the home. Inadequate encouragement has been given to any desire for higher education, at secondary, trade or technical school. It is time this narrow tradition was broken. The girls should be encouraged to seek training in accordance with their natural desires and abilities and they should be sent out of the Hollies for this having either daily, or if necessary, permanently to billets'. Boys were still trained for a trade during school hours, but payment to them was being considered. The question was raised whether or not the children had sufficient freedom 'to leave the estate, and whether or not the sexes mix as much as desirable'.

In 1946 there was an exchange holiday of eight boys with boys from the Schaerbeck Town Ophanage in Belgium.

There was a long discussion in 1946 over whether children should stay on at school until 16. The managing committee wanted to extend their leaving age, and cited the view of the education minister that he wished to extend the school leaving age to 16. It was pointed out by the education officer that, 'Children who have been brought up in the atmosphere of an institution for any length of time learn to adapt themselves more readily to a normal life if placed out before rather than after 16'.

It was also noted that children starting work at 16 would be working beside others who had not come from an institution, who entered employment at 14 and who would receive higher wages.

Differentiation in wages would no doubt accentuate the sense of inferiority which, generally speaking, children from a residential school feel because of their training and experience. 'This children have when they compare themselves with those brought up in a normal home environment'.

If wage differentials were based on age, employers would choose the younger worker rather than an older worker who had two extra years of schooling but was similarly inexperienced. Also, some occupations like the post office and army bands closed recruitment at 16. This was a good example of how difficult it can be to bring in even an obviously beneficial reform in a localised area. The managing committee decided to deal with each case separately and allow children who wanted to and had the ability to stay until 16. The national school leaving age was not raised to 16 for another twenty years; it was raised from 14 to 15 in 1947.

In 1948 a report from the Superintendent said, 'I have been able, in the case of new admissions, to keep boys and girls together in the same homes. So far the experiment has proved to be successful'.

Under instructions for arrival of children at the homes in 1946 the reception staff were told, 'Let it definitely and clearly be made manifest what the governing aspect symbolises: friendliness, protection, safety, brightness and consideration and a kindly atmosphere, and if it is a wayward child, it is still a home for him'.

'First impressions are important: the child is suffering from great emotional strain by estrangement from home, parents and the old familiar faces and surroundings. It experiences fear. Parents or friends leave him manifesting sorrow and distress'. A memorandum advised that children 'should come in the mornings to a bright room. Tastefully decorated toys and a bowl of goldfish, etc., should be provided in the reception room. Such an atmosphere would impress itself on the child's mind and allay suspicion and fear'.

A welfare officer at a similar establishment, Shirley Oaks children's home in Croydon, wrote on 8 March 1949:

> There is still a great deal to be done in making home visits to gain a clear insight into the family background, so as to assist the children who build up a defence against their feelings and longings, and others who show their sufferings in outward behaviour. It is so essential to try and keep the children in

contact with their relations. Unfortunately, many of those children in most need of personal affection and reassurance are frequently those who have developed the most difficult behavioural traits and therefore least acceptable. Contact must always be maintained between them through the Child Welfare Officer, with the agreement and co-operation of the foster parent.

Like most theoretical arrangements which relied on goodwill, this would break down easily, in some cases leaving children not knowing if they even had siblings who had been fostered, or even adopted while they stayed in care.

Enuretic children were boarded out as Dr Bricknell was 'of the opinion that an enuretic child is more likely to be cured in a foster home than an institution'. Of 82 admissions in the quarter ended in June 1943, 26 were verminous.

6

The 1950s

At Christmas 1950, 107 children were away with 'aunts and uncles', and 61 children were on home leave with relatives. It was not necessarily easy to find willing 'aunts and uncles'. The Welfare Officer reported in May 1953 that since they were admitted in January, three boys, aged 12 and 13, had had no visitors. 'I shall try to find them

Willow Cottage, June 1949.

53

friends, but as it has been pointed out previously, it is difficult to find contacts for the older children, especially as they frequently have problems of one sort or another and require very understanding 'aunts and uncles'.

A Home Office memorandum of 1951 gave explicit instructions on the reception of children: 'The housemother should have full information about the child before he comes, so that he can be greeted by name and made to feel he is not a stranger . . . On arrival he should be shown around the home and, if he has a brother or sister or friend there, he should see him at once. Children should be allowed to bring with them any personal possessions to which they are attached and these should be treated with respect'.

A Home Office circular of 1951 recommended children of all ages to be living in the same house, with at least one baby, with a housefather who would go out to work; and a housemother who would

The Hogan family: (left to right), Colin, Veronica, Michael, David (his 'Account'
on page 146) and Pat (kneeling), at The Hollies Sports Day, summer 1960.

stay at home, in an idealised picture of what family life should be. It does not seem to have been tried at the Hollies and is impractical, anyway, but is an interesting pointer towards the direction childcare was taking: away from Institutions and towards fostering.

The officer wrote on 7 May 1954, 'at present many of the children who require "aunts and uncles" are either teenage girls with behaviour difficulties or boys, while a large proportion of the applications received for potential outside contacts are for small girls'.

In September 1956, 65 discharges were reported in the previous month or so: 40 to parents; 1 to another school or home, 4 to hospital; 7 on holiday; 4 were boarded out (fostered) and 9 to work and after care. The weekly cost of keeping a child at The Hollies in 1959-60 was £9.0s.7d. In the year 1961-2 there was 330 children and 68 staff.

Some of the outdoor games included tennis swimming, sports practice and netball. Indoor activities were gymnastics, billiards, table tennis, darts and ring nets, dominoes, playing cards, chess, draughts, snakes and ladders; and the reading and writing room. Children were also engaged in badminton, dancing and singing classes and scripture classes.

Discipline and Order

When the managing committee was investigating the claim of a girl that had been hit by a housemother, the woman defended herself by remarking that slapping the children was commonplace. The managing committee told the Superintendent to call the Housemothers together. They announced, 'it has come to the attention of the managing committee that children in the cottages have been slapped by housemothers; that this practice must cease; and that the managing committee will take a very serious view of any infraction of the punishment rules in future'.

From the 1950s the character of the home changed for a number of reasons: in the nation as a whole there was general social change with the disappearance of an agreed common set of social values; a drastic decline in the morale of staff; and the increasing proportion of children sent to the Home from the courts.

The Superintendent reported on 17 July 1953 a catalogue of offences: a number of children damaging the gardens of residents; three boys absconding and one of them charged with stealing £65; four girls appearing before Bromley Juvenile Court on a charge of larceny from local shops. There was also a report of two senior girls absconding and appearing at Dartford Juvenile Court charged with larceny.

The Superintendent went on to say 'the admission of children who have appeared before Juvenile Courts and proved guilty of stealing and habitual truancy is not altogether satisfactory in the case of the Hollies which being of an entirely "open" nature where children all have to go to school and church, offers temptation to such children which they are not able to overcome'.

'Unfortunately such children nearly always involve other children who would never otherwise have contemplated such acts. I submit as my opinion that the majority of CYPA (Children and Young Persons Act) children would be better placed in an establishment where the school is on the premises and consequently a firmer discipline and greater supervision might be maintained. They all need on admission a period of firm discipline and training before coming to The Hollies where of necessity one has to rely on their trustworthiness and honour.'

There was no change in policy and September 1955 had him again addressing the management committee with the serious case of a 14-year-old girl, who 'had a very bad influence over other girls, and led several of them astray with her. I even had complaints from the workman employed by contractors at the Hollies, regarding her disgraceful language and improper suggestions. I desire to report that in my opinion, the admission of children of this age, whose previous record of behaviour has been so bad, cannot but have an unfortunate influence on other children, and on the general tone of the behaviour of the children as a whole'. In December 1956 there were 334 children on the roll, of whom 55 were sent there by the courts under the Children and Young Person's Act.

Many children were short-stay children. An LCC publication of 1962 called *In London's Care* noted that 12,000 applications were made a year for children to go into care. 'The temporary illness or confinement of a mother gives rise to more applications than any other single cause, and about half the children received into care in a recent year came into the Council "family" for that reason'.

Other reasons why children came into care included: children abandoned by their mother, (father not living with family), or unable to care for children, permanent disability of parent or guardian, parent or guardian suffering from mental disorder (within the meaning of the Mental Health Act 1959) which renders him unfit to have the care of children (Section (48) II (a) of the Children and Young Persons Act 1963), parent or guardian in prison or remanded in custody, family homeless because of eviction, unsatisfactory home conditions.

Staff morale was also affected by the difficult children. There were staff shortages because of the long hours and the financial attractions of other employment. A new Superintendent (the former deputy) was appointed in July 1959. The children's officer of the LCC reported in November 1964 'as a result of the good relationship which he has built up and the popularity of his appointment, he quickly rallied the staff around him and The Hollies moved into a period of much needed modernisation and improvement. He can look with pride on what has been achieved in recent years at The Hollies in a particularly difficult phase, largely due to a succession of staff changes and a grave shortage of qualified and experienced staff. In

Boisterous short-stay infants.

Swimming – a popular activity at the Homes' own well-appointed swimming pool.

addition there had been a substantial increase in the number of disturbed children admitted to The Hollies leading to difficulties both within the establishment and with the local schools'.

'The final problem The Hollies had to face was the change in society around them. To pick two examples of the sort of events which had not been recorded earlier: on 14 January 1959 two sisters were delivering party invitations to friends nearby. A man stopped in a car and offered them a lift. He drove them to a lane in Chislehurst and said they should undress. They refused and he started to undress himself. They screamed and he said he would take them home if they were quiet. He drove them to a road nearby and let them out unharmed. On 23 September 1960 the nurse Sister Davies woke in her room in the infirmary to find a drunken man with a large carving knife in her bedroom, 'she dealt with him in a very calm and courageous manner' and help was summoned. There was no damage to Sister Davies or the children in the infirmary and he was given a six months' jail sentence.

Children's mental health became increasingly important. A report on adolescence in 1961 remarked on 'the need as adolescence approaches, to satisfy the demand for more detailed and accurate information about the child's early life; to consider how best a store of personal and family details can be built up, even if some of them are distressing to satisfy the longing, so widely felt for an authentic background'.

The whole of Palm household, comprising 20 boys and three staff, went to Luxembourg for a week in August 1963. In June 1965 children went to see Ali Baba on Ice at Wembley, arranged by the *Daily Mirror* Uncles Club. Children were given half a crown each by their 'uncles' and used it going to see Snow White at Bromley.

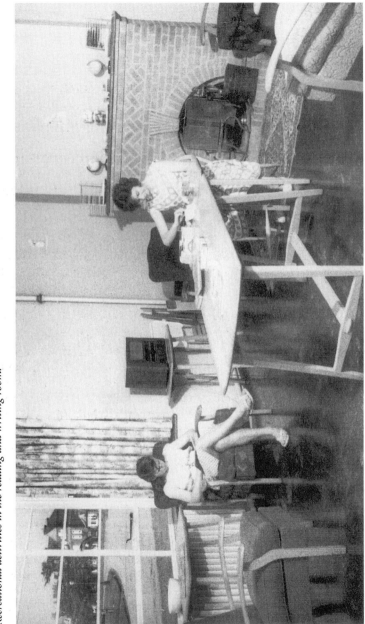

Recreational activities in the reading and writing room.

7

London Borough of Southwark

Southwark Council took over the administration of the Hollies in 1965. The post of matron disappeared and some house parents were referred to by their first names or as 'uncle' or 'auntie'. House parents now had much more control over the children, making decisions about where they should go to school.

The children were given their own money to spend outside the homes and were sometimes sent out to the shops by house parents, older children bought their own clothes. Some of these reforms were already underway when Southwark took over but the borough consolidated them.

While Southwark Council took the major decisions regarding the Hollies, the Social Services Committee would also take an interest in activities at the Hollies. For example Councillor H.W. Hinds, chairman of the committee reported in 1966 on 'the success of a team entered from The Hollies in the annual Adventure Trophy competition organised by the London Federation for Boys' Clubs. The team met strong competition from rival teams such as Police Cadets and similar groups whose members included young men up to 19 years of age.' The Hollies received a sword in commemoration and individual team members received gold medals.

By the mid 1960s, nine of the twelve newly formed Inner London boroughs had an increase in the number of children being received into residential care, not least among children from African/Caribbean origin and heritage. One reason for this increase was that parents from a different ethnic heritage were less likely to have an extended family living in London, (unlike people who were more established here; who may have had more resources to fall back upon if problems occurred). Ironically children that were in care of inner London councils, like Southwark, were placed in children's homes outside their boroughs, in towns such as Sidcup. These factors caused some unease not only for children living at the Hollies perhaps temporarily in an environment different from that to which they had been accustomed in London. Equally, many people already residing in Sidcup and the surrounding area may have had their suspicion aroused, not only by unfamiliar faces but because many children came from ethnic backgrounds in a district where the population were white and middle class. Some unease and mistrust existed because some people of the community had the attitude that these children must have done something fundamentally wrong. Even with the best intentions, some people misunderstood why these children were placed in public care in the first place.

Statistically, we are writing about an age when it was considered that the longer a child was in care, the greater the probability they would remain in residential care for the whole of their childhood. Although the Hollies was a home identified for long term care, it also had children in short and medium term care. During the middle 1960s most local authorities witnessed an increasing number of children coming into care each month. Southwark Council in common with many other Inner London authorities didn't have enough accommodation within their borough to fulfil all the care orders that were issued. In an attempt to respond to this demand Southwark Council embarked on building new accommodation within

Recreational facilities beside Oaks House, autumn 1961.

their borough as well as building new facilities at the Hollies.

John Mercier a teacher recalled: 'From 1957 to 1968 I taught at Hurstmere Boys' School. We used to get a number of the boys in the 11–16 age range attending the school. The Headmaster, Mr Watts, had a policy of school uniform, so we never knew who was from the Hollies until we got to know some of them. One or two were tough nuts and one or two were problem pupils in terms of either behaviour or low ability or BOTH! But it was a good policy to accept them on the same terms as all the others. In fact Mr Watts never let his staff have access to the records that used to come up with all the entrants from junior school so that the new boys could make a fresh start and the teachers find out for themselves what the abilities and behaviour were. Of course this did not apply to entrants who had an illness record such as epilepsy or asthma'.

On the 4 June 1966 James Callaghan MP officially opened three new buildings: a reception centre, an assessment home and a boys' hostel that was aligned to Halfway Street. The assessment centre catered for the needs of children that were either coming into care for the first time, or whose foster placement, sometimes even adoption, had broken down. Primarily, it was a place where children would stay before decisions would be made about their future and what short of care would be suitable for that child.

The reception centre looked after children who had a care order placed on them by the courts. The boys' hostel hoped to provide a greater degree of independence for teenagers preparing to leave local authority care. All these establishments had a medium to high level of staff support.

In the early 1970s Southwark Council embarked on a costly refurbishment scheme on most of the houses on the site costing hundreds of thousands of pounds. The outhouses were converted into staff accommodation.

Staff sometimes had problems of their own. Two tragedies occurred among the staff at the Hollies in the early 1970s. Late in 1970 a residential social worker took his own life two days before he was to face criminal charges alleging indecency against three boys in care. In June 1972, Les Lewis, acting head of the children's home, hanged himself in the Hollies woods behind the Office. It was stated at the inquest, 'an accumulation of circumstances', including a divorce and financial problems had led to him taking his own life.

Battle With the Lamorbey West Residents' Association

With the increase in fostering, which took what fieldwork social workers considered the most adaptable children out of the homes, there was a larger proportion of difficult children resident. Inevitably this cause problems in relations with the neighbouring community. The *Sidcup Times* of 3 May 1973 reported a 'Bid to Oust 'Nuisance' Children'. The Lamorbey West Residents' Association was campaigning for the closure of The Hollies, arguing that children from the homes were responsible for crime and bullying in the area.

With a 1,500 membership, the Residents were reported to be

'campaigning for the closure of "The Hollies", the 45 acre site occupied by Southwark Council for housing children "in care". They claim that many of the children there some of whom are on remand, are a nuisance to the community. When the matter was raised at the association's meeting last week, guest speaker Councillor Brian Forrest, of Harcourt Avenue, Sidcup, was urged to fight for a compulsory purchase order to be placed on the land. He promised to investigate. Vice-Chairman of the Residents Association, W. Winter of Haddon Grove, Blackfen, claimed the land could be used for Bexley housing, social amenities and more schools. He felt the association should intervene to get the present use ended. At present 150 children are at "The Hollies". Accommodation for another 58 is being planned, including homes for 19 subnormal adolescents some of it in Hollies houses. Residents claim the police attribute 70 per cent of juvenile crime in the area are from children in the homes and allege four out of ten cases, at Dartford Juvenile Court come from "The Hollies".

It is understood that moves are already "in the pipeline" for Bexley Council to approach Southwark Council. They wish to negotiate "peacefully" for at least some of this open space to build a new school'.

Comments from residents this week included

'Residents Association Committee member Mr George Rich: There are other homes of similar or near similar nature in the area, some deal with sub-normal children. This is too many for one district and they are too near private houses. V. Beagles of Blackfen said, 'I have heard personally of six break-ins in the area this year as well as an attempted theft at my home. There may be others'. Mrs A. French of Wymcham Avenue, Blackfen: 'My 11-year-old daughter could not attend school through bullying by a Hollies child at the same school. She was covered with bruises and I had to keep her home for safety of the recommendations of the headmaster. A second time she was given a black eye by a Hollies child'.

'Susan Connolly of Haddon Grove, Blackfen said :
   The children are rough and tough in order to survive, but Southwark Council should make it public knowledge that remand children are housed there, very few residents are aware of this. The rise of delinquency in Blackfen is alarming and could be a bad influence on other children.
   Nevertheless I thought often that the buildings and open spaces at the Hollies are not being used to their full potential. I think that homes could be erected at the Hollies to accommodate the homeless of Bexley, especially young couples who cannot buy homes of their own. But not withstanding this, the children in there must be our number one priority'.

The following week, on 10 May 1973, The Hollies made the *Sidcup Times* again under the headline ' "Treat us as equals" plead children in care':
   'A heart searching letter from the children, signed by two of them, (whose names are with the editor) asks the residents to give them a fair break. They write:
   'Why do we have to be labelled as a nuisance, while other children in Sidcup can behave as they wish, and by their delinquent behaviour affect our lives?
   Are we unacceptable because the basic knowledge of our past nudges the social conscience of the locals, or is it they are jealous of the better standards which are maintained in the majority of cases, by the Hollies kids.
   Most of us are proud to live in Sidcup, and are happy to be able to do so, why should people only be able to see the bad in us and not really knowing us, pass judgement on us all on

the basis of the attitudes and actions of a small minority.

We are sure that the views printed in the last issue are the views of only a small minority group. We are not a menace to local society – more likely we are a complement. So why cannot we be allowed to live in what to most of us, is the only home we know? The majority of us are hurt and annoyed that what we thought was a happy home has become now so sad and miserable.'

'Backing the children are two residents, Mrs T. C. Claydon, of Kimberley Drive, Sidcup, writes:

These children have many difficulties with which to cope, not only within their own families and residential establishments, but also with the attitudes of local people. It seems these attitudes polarise from the extreme of sickly sentimentality to that so condemning them as juvenile delinquents. As a social worker may I suggest that before criticising behaviour these people ask themselves how their children would react to the stress of being separated from their family and placed in a strange environment. It may be unfortunate that so many children in care are concentrated in one area, but I suggest that the ones who suffer from this arrangement are the children, who experience prejudice from the community.

Mr Jeremiah O'Sullivan, of Burnt Oak Lane, Sidcup, writes:

It is said that in our so-called advanced age, children in care, the result of broken homes, should be branded publicly as nuisance children. They are really society's unfortunate ones, forsaken and abandoned by their very own.'

'The Hollies and such establishments exist only for these children. They do not need sympathy; they need people who really care and people who are understanding of their deep emotional hurt and their basic insecurity.

The children need our understanding and not our condemnation and our wrath. There are many dedicated people who give their lives for the welfare of the children. But sadly there are not enough who care and not enough who can persevere in such trying work. If local residents cannot stand the existence of these children at the Hollies, then what are the proposals? Occasionally some of these children may be misplaced and placed in the wrong kind of home, but usually nowadays, there are homes for all categories of deprived children'.

A week later the newspaper reported under the headline: 'Increase in number at the Hollies' that 'Lamorbey East Residents Association wrote to the Home Office Town Clerk and Chief Executive Officer of Southwark Borough Council this week to complain that during recent years there has been an increased number of remand children housed at the Hollies. They feel many local people are convinced there is a connection between the petty crime in the area and remand children from the Home. The association has strongly complained against the misuse of the homes for deprived non-delinquent children. A protest to the Home Office that children from the Hollies appear to be allowed to roam the streets to the alarm of the elderly people was also featured by the association in a letter to the assistant principal of the Homes requesting better discipline and a curfew hour for the children.

To mark Queen's Silver Jubilee in 1977, the Hollies hosted a 5-a-side football competition. The competition was open to any team that wanted to compete. There were two cup contests; one for boys under sixteen years and the other for adults. In the evening there was a dance held in the gym for children, staff and friends in attendance.

The Bitter End
No records are publicly available for the time from 1965 when the London Borough of Southwark took over the Hollies but it suffered an accelerating decline; hastened by the twin policies of fostering as many children as possible; and having children's homes as part of the community. This meant when a new housing estate would be built, for example, a children's home would be built with it; or a large family house would be purchased, looking no different from others in the street, and it would be converted into a children's home for a small number of children. Obviously this was very different from the ethos which had informed The Hollies and such an approach was not compatible with the running of a home that kept children separate from the community.

In 1982 it was announced that the Hollies would cease functioning as a children's home, on a planned closure over three to five years. There were chronic staff shortages and pressures on the remaining staff to cover unfilled vacancies. In 1983 there were approximately 60 children on the site.

Staff problems were a curse to childcare, in particular a high staff turnover due to the low remuneration this testing work attracted. There was also an increasing tendency in the 1970s and 1980s for the administration to set its own priorities, and for some staff to look to their own interests, neither paying due regard to the interests of the children in public residential care. This led to what has fairly been called the lowest point in the history of childcare, which happened at The Hollies.

During the first three years of 1980s, about 70% of the children from the Hollies that attended the Burnt Oak Primary had behavioural difficulties. Some children were aggressive and violent; this caused disruption in the children's education. Others were withdrawn and emotionally disturbed, and consequently had problems relating to both other children and teachers. When children regularly arrived late for school in the morning, usually they would be from the Home, and accompanied by their carers. The majority of children who displayed such behaviour were likely to be children recently received into care or in-care short term. Sometimes Burnt Oak School would be notified early in morning by telephone to expect a new pupil from the Hollies and this could cause further problems trying to settle them into a new school and environment. Such circumstances could prove problematic.

In 1983 there had been a long dispute between Southwark and care staff about hours and rates of pay. Residential care staff had refused to stay on duty at nights and weekends to look after the 33 children who were now at the homes. Southwark was sending non-union staff and outside social workers to supervise the children between 6.30 in the evening and 7.15 the next morning when the regular staff returned.

Understandably, the children resented being treated this way and resolved to make a protest. When their night 'minders' arrived on 26 October 1983 the children barricaded themselves into their homes. The following night, with no warning, a number of social workers arrived and ordered all the children out, giving them no time even to pick up a toothbrush. The children resisted and police were called.

Twenty children were taken to Bexleyheath police station and eighteen ran away, five of them for four days. The police searched the house for the runaways, breaking down the locked doors of the bedrooms, and council workers arrived to strip the home of its furniture and the children's belongings – supposedly to return to them in the new children's homes they would be sent to, where staff were not in dispute over pay and conditions.

A reporter from *The Times* described the scene later, 'The house presented a dismal picture yesterday, as though ransacked by burglars. Three of the children had made their way back to look for cherished possessions and they wandered through the empty rooms in disbelief'.

It was reported in the *Sidcup Times* on 18 November 1983, that the former Prime Minister Mr Edward Heath, requested an inquiry into the removal of 33 children from the Hollies. In a 207-page report published in January 1985, Southwark's chief executive, Gerry Corless, blamed councillors' conflict of interests for helping flare-up the riots at the Hollies in 1983. The report was critical of the trade union Nalgo and claiming they put their sympathies with residential social workers above their duties to look after the children. It was a tragic end to the life of a once proud institution.

The Hollies reopened as a residential home, although the number of children there was curtailed, amid claims that staff were paid to do nothing.

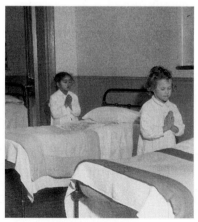

Bedtime prayers.

Accounts
from Former Residents

ᔆ THE SIDCUP HOMES MAGAZINE ᔆ

128, CLAPHAM ROAD, S.W.9.

20th October, 1929.

DEAR MR. OCKENDEN,

It was a great surprise to me to receive the "Homes' Magazine" once again, which was very acceptable, after all these years.

I must thank you for editing such a fine book, to keep the old boys in touch with one another. I have used the other one you so kindly sent on to Walter, whom no doubt you will hear from in the near future. Please find enclosed 2s. P.O. for same.

It may interest you to know that I have a collection of the old Magazines, dating from No. 1, March, 1911, to No. 20, March, 1916. In looking through some of the old numbers, you give a Roll of Honour of those serving in His Majesty's forces. Some of these names are very familiar to me. Where are they now? Could we not have a real Old Boys' Gathering next Whitsun Monday with some of the old boys who left in 1903-4-5?

I for one would certainly make an effort to attend such a gathering.

Will now close, wishing the Magazine every success.

Yours sincerely,

P. J. BAKER.

Early Accounts
from Former Residents

199, CLAPHAM PARK ROAD,
CLAPHAM, S.W.4.

DEAR MR. OCKENDEN,

Many thanks for the "Sidcup Homes Magazine." The contents satisfied my curiosity to know what dear old Sidcup has been doing since I left. The improvements that have taken place are staggering to one who was there over 20 years ago, and must be a revelation to many other old boys when they read the Magazine. When I read about the Fair Day, Cash Discs and the holiday by the sea, one paused to think of the joy it would have brought to us old boys to have spent even one day by the sea. I never saw the sea until I could afford a holiday three years after having left Sidcup.

My spare copy I have sent out to Charles, as I know he will be pleased to see it. Enclosed is 3s., so please send a few more copies, as I intend hunting out a few old boys to keep the pot boiling.

Congratulations are due to you for the able way you have edited our first number.

Yours sincerely,

ARCHIE RICHARDSON.

Personal Accounts of Life at The Hollies

The following are accounts of children in care.
The dates are of the time they were in the Sidcup Homes.

ROSE LLOYDS 1915–1928

Rose Lloyds as a middle-aged woman needed some official certification of her birth, as her birth was never registered, so she wrote to the London County Council who replied on 16 May 1962:

LONDON COUNTY COUNCIL
The County Hall Westminster Bridge
London S. E. 1.

16 May, 1962

Dear Madam

A search has been made in the records of the Greenwich Board of Guardians, now in my custody here. I have pleasure in giving you the following information:- Name – Rose M. Harris Born – April or August, 1911 (exact date and place not stated) Admitted to Greenwich Infirmary, aged 2, 10 September, 1913 Transferred finally to Greenwich Institution, 1 September, 1914 Transferred to Sidcup Home, 26 July, 1915 Discharged to Service, 24 July, 1928. Father – George T. Harris, of 23 Giffin Street in 1914 Mother – Rose Harris Brother George, born 1905 As I understand that you cannot obtain a birth certificate I suggest that you keep this letter carefully to use in the future as evidence of your age and identity for official purposes such as employment, pension, etc.

Yours faithfully,
for Clerk of the Council

I lived in Mulberry Cottage with a wonderful mulberry tree on the green, such a friendly tree. In the spring, birds seemed to come from nowhere to sing. Teachers from our school would come to pick the tender leaves for their silkworms. The mulberries came in abundance. I had many a stomach ache from eating the fruit before it was ripe, but mulberries went down so well when we were so hungry. Of course, this was strictly forbidden. If we were caught we would be punished, maybe a whole weekend in confinement with very little food. In the autumn when the leaves fell we  would have great fun running through them while sweeping them up. In the winter, although bare, it was still there, big and strong.

Years later, I went back to see the children who then lived in Mulberry Cottage and the tree was gone. I was told that a foster mother, who had only stayed for six months, had had it cut down. To her the leaves had been too much clearing up. I felt I had lost a dear friend of my childhood.

As I remember . . . I was wearing a red velvet dress, and holding tight to a lady's hand. I was four years old and this day is very clear in my mind. I was about to enter the Poor Law Institution run by Greenwich and Deptford Board of Guardians.

We came to some very large iron gates. The lady rang the bell and a man came out to unlock the gates and let us in. Bang went the gates behind us. We were taken into a room known as the gatehouse. A woman in a nurse's uniform came in. She asked the lady to leave. I started to scream and scream. I didn't want her to go. I was so frightened and then was very sick. I was told later that the lady had been my mother – I never saw her again from that day to this. And on that awful day I started my life in the Poor Law Institution.

We lived in Cottages, 15 children (all girls) to a cottage. We didn't see the boys in the Home as boys and girls were kept apart. There was a school in the home grounds beside the big iron gates that locked out the rest of the world. The girls and boys had separate playgrounds, well fenced round so neither could meet, but there were small peepholes cut in the fence just big enough to see a face through. One day – just by chance – I heard a boy call my name: 'Rose, Rose, come to the fence. I am your brother. My name is

George'. That was the first time I ever knew I had a brother. I saw him many times through the hole in the fence, but only on Christmas Day were we allowed to meet and have tea together.

The foster mothers in each cottage were very strict. I had many a whipping with the back of a hair brush until I was black and blue. I spent many a weekend in bed for punishment with very little to eat and sometimes I was forgotten altogether. I would have nightmares. I would sleepwalk, looking for my mother. I would wake up scream-ing almost every night, well into my adult life. Army friends even now reminisce and laugh about how when, in the ATS during the war, my screams disturbed them more than Hitler's bombs. And many a time I've scared the wits out of my husband as my screams made him jump half out of bed before he'd even woken up. Needless to say, both my brother and I suffer from inferiority complexes.

I don't want anyone to think that my early life had no highlights and that I always felt let down. There were happy times, when we children made our own fun. Also folks not connected with the running of the Poor Law Institution would give us presents and parties at Christmas, which stand out well in my memory. The nurses in the Infirmary were very kind and so were the teachers at the school. I well remember the teachers would bring in their stale cake and cut it into small pieces so each of us could have a little. Some of the children were visited on a Saturday afternoon by relatives and friends from two o'clock until four o'clock, but none ever came to see me. I cannot remember this worrying me too much, I looked for-ward to it as some of the children had sweets to share.

The Home was situated in one of the most beautiful parts of Kent, not that any of us, at that time appreciated it. It was a vast area, of countryside with trees, fields, lawns, gardens. All our cottages were named after trees in alphabetical order. They went like this: Acacia, Almond, Cedar, Chestnut, Elder, Elm, Hawthorn, Hazel, Laburnum, Laurel, Lilac, Maple, Mulberry, Myrtle, Olive, Palm, Pine, Poplar, Rowan, Sycamore. Each cottage had its appropriate tree on the lawn near the cottage. Those were the girls' cottages with 15 girls in each, all ages from four years to sixteen years. The boys' houses were known as blocks which were much larger and held many more boys in each block. They were also named after trees. There were five of them: the Oaks, the Limes, the Firs, the Beeches and Ash. The main building, where the master of the Home lived was called the Hollies, but we didn't go near there if we could help it. Of course there was a house where matron lived, too, and an Infirmary. There was a water tower with a large clock at the top. The laundry was there. There was a bakery where all the bread was made, a gymnasium, a swimming pool, a school. So it was almost self-contained, though there was no church so most services would be held in the School Hall. Sometimes we went to the church in the town where some of the boys sang in the choir.

The vegetables were grown in the grounds. We would see the horses and the ploughmen at work in the fields. As soon as the foster mother saw the horses around she would send us out with a bucket and shovel to go round the grounds to collect the horse manure for her garden. We hated that job. Root vegetables were mostly grown. We seemed to live on swedes, carrots, turnips, beetroot and potatoes. On Saturday we sometimes had cabbage with a hot meal. We had cold mutton on Sunday as no cooking was done on Sunday. I can't ever remember having salad, apart from when there was a glut of lettuce grown. We would have that on Sunday, with our cold meat and beet-root. Two or three of us would be sent to the outhouse on Saturday to wash the lettuce ready for Sunday. If anyone had passed the out-house at that time they would have thought we were rabbits. Lettuce is lovely when you are hungry.

A horse and cart brought milk round daily in large urns to each cottage. We would have to take out enamel jugs to be filled. In the summer time all milk was put on the stove to boil and the foster mother would leave it to get cold, then take the cream off the top. We never saw where that went. We always had fish on Fridays and Ash Wednesday to start Lent. Oh, that awful boiled cod, how we hated it! Horses and carts were used for all deliveries of food rations to each cottage. The only car I ever saw at that time belonged to the doctor who came in when needed and twice a week on routine.

We were all vaccinated as I suppose all children were at that time. We had four pricks at the top of the left arm and they came up like four large scars. Very painful. The arm was wrapped up with lots of lint and bandage. We cried a lot with the pain, until the scabs start-ed to form, which were as large as our one pence piece. Then we had to be careful the scabs were not knocked off before they were ready. We were all left with four large scars, which we take to the grave. I'm pleased my daughter did not have to suffer so, when she was vaccinated.

We loved the Harvest Festivals which were held in the School Hall. The Harvest hymns were well known by us all. We would sing at the top of our voices, 'We plough the fields and scatter, The good seed on the land, But it is fed and watered, By God's Almighty Hand,' and 'All things bright and beautiful, All creatures great and small, All things wise and wonderful, The Lord God made them all.' It would lift our hearts to heaven.

All around us (but out of reach) were large vegetables, wonderful roses, apples, pears, Michaelmas daisies, in large jars. Everything had been grown in the Home and it would be given to the hospitals in the town. At that time there was a Cottage Hospital and Queen Mary's Hospital. There wasn't a Health Service those days and to us it seemed the right place for it to go.

When I was eight years old I caught mumps and was put in the Infirmary. One evening I was told to look out of the window and wave goodbye to my brother as he was being sent to Canada. He was 15 years old. I didn't know what this meant, but I waved goodbye. I didn't know I wouldn't see him again for fourteen years. 24 other boys were going as well. They were promised the Good Life. What they didn't say about this Promised Land was that task-masters would work him to a standstill, and that he'd have to combat the  raw tyranny of the seasons, the loneliness of the long evenings in a strange house in a strange land with no friends, beyond the reach of any kind of love or affection. He would on many a night cry himself to sleep. He was put on a farm owned by a Mr and Mrs Dickie. They put him to work from four o'clock in the morning until sunset. He has told me since that he had to do the family wash, clean the house and work on the farm, wages being next to nothing. He eventually earned the respect of his employers, had a family and bought a home.

I didn't see my brother again while I was in the house, though I had many letters and at Christmas he would send me one of his hard earned dollars.

What stands out most in my mind at this time was always being so hungry and cold. Food was very meagre, two thin slices of bread and treacle for breakfast and tea. I can see the mutton stew now on the plate at dinner time, swimming in fat, and lumps of swede floating around in it. We were so hungry we would eat it and be very sick afterwards. I spent my school life watching the hall clock, waiting for it to point to twelve o'clock dinnertime. When we said grace, I would have one eye open in case the girl next to me pinched my one and only potato. When the house mother had her breakfast she had fried bacon, and we would stand behind her to see which one of us could get the bacon rind from her plate first. We took it in turns after a while. We children only had fried bacon on Christmas Day and an egg on Easter Sunday.

All through the year we strip-washed in cold water in very cold rooms. I can see the ice-covered windows now. There was one room with a coal fire in the winter, but we were never allowed by the fire. One morning stands out in my mind still. One of the girls, my age – we were friends – was very sick, and as we were sick very often the foster-mother didn't take any notice. That night she was very bad and the next day she died of meningitis. It took me a long while getting over that.

Religion played a big part in our lives. A text from a religious calendar had to be learned every morning before breakfast. The Sunday Collect had to be learned by heart before breakfast every Sunday. I still know most of them. And God help us if we didn't know what prayer-book Sunday it was. I would get muddled, and still do, with Septuagesima, Sexagesima and Quinquagesima, but it had to be right. We had to learn not only the Collect, but also the Epistle and Gospel during the day, answering questions on them in the evening. I found them very hard to remember. There had been so much going on in the day. On Sundays we had to keep so clean and tidy and so holy and silent out of fear of the foster mother and punishment.

We would have a morning service in the school hall taken by a very old clergyman, whom some of the boys at the other side of the hall would make fun of and then get punished for it. It wasn't a very bright service and the sermon seemed very long. I never could understand it. I was hoping all the time he would hurry up and end so we could go back to dinner which would be cold mutton and dry bread as there was no cooking on Sunday. In the afternoon we would be taken in twos behind each other to the local church. We felt the lowest of the low, sitting on one side of the church with all outside people, as we called them, sitting on the other side of the church in their grand clothes. We always felt their children held their noses far too high in the air when they looked at us.

Matron would walk up and down the pews to look for good girls whom she would give a penny or a halfpenny to put in the collection bag. When she came to or near me I would sit up straight and look holy in hopes she wouldn't pass me by. Then the Sunday came – my heart leaped – she gave me a penny to put in the bag. I hoped the outside people were seeing that I was rich enough to give a whole penny to the church, which I thought must have been very poor to want of children who never saw a penny, which they had held in their hand for such a short time. It couldn't be for the clergyman. He was big and fat and very well fed. My hopes were dashed to the ground on the following Monday morning at school. The teacher was talking about giving and said that when Matron gave us our money to put in the church collection, God knew it was not from us, as we didn't have it. Oh, how pleased God must have been with Matron. After tea, which sometimes we had with some very burnt seed cake, being Sunday, we had another service where whoever was called had to answer questions on the Epistle and Gospel which could be a dreaded nightmare. I remember it still. Best part of Sunday for us was later in the evening when we had hymn singing and, not being allowed to talk, we all let rip. My favourite was: 'The day Thou gavest, Lord, is ended'.

We worked very hard, rising at quarter to six in the morning. Before going to school we would have to polish and scrub floors, and black-lead the coal-stove. After our dinner we cleaned cutlery and pots and pans, which had to be bright and shining. Evenings we would have to sit on forms, darn our stockings, patch our clothes and knit our own black stockings when we could darn our old ones no more.

In between school times we spent many hours on our knees not necessarily praying, though we had to do a great deal of that, but scrubbing and polishing and gardening. So very early in life I learned to pray the Kitchen Prayer:

> Lord of pots and pans and things, Since I've no time to be
> A saint in doing lovely things, Or watching late with Thee,
> Or dreaming in the dawn light Or storming Heaven's gates;
> Make me a saint, dear Lord, By getting meals and washing up
>   the plates.
> Although I must have Martha's hands, I have a Mary mind,
> And when I black the boots and shoes Thy sandals, Lord, I find;
> I think of how they trod the earth Each time I scrub the floor.
> Accept this meditation, Lord, I haven't time for more.

I wasn't ill very often, but I did have to go every morning to the Infirmary to have my ears cleaned as they discharged all the time. I wasn't alone; nearly all of us had to go to Outpatient for something or other. It was always full, the room we waited in. I sometimes wondered if it was such a room where the roof would open, as in Jesus' time, and a bed would come through the roof. But, of course, it never did.

As I got older I suffered from very large, painful boils on my chin, under the arms, between the legs, and on my bottom so I couldn't sit down. At one time when I was really suffering badly, and the foster mother got really nasty with me to make me work. She came with a stick to get me out of bed as her room had a small window looking out on my bed and she saw I wasn't up. I moved as quickly as I could to get away from her, and I couldn't stop crying, I was in such pain. When I got to the Infirmary Outpatients, I was in such a state, the nurse said I was to see the doctor (who had come in that day). The doctor said I was to stay in the Infirmary. Oh, what bliss. The nurses were so kind and gentle with my boils. At that time the only treatment was very hot fomentation to bring the core out. It took a long time to get better. I was in the Infirmary four weeks, but to me it was heaven. The nurses gave us nice things to eat, such as pat-a-cake biscuits, and cocoa with sugar in it for supper, unheard of in Mulberry Cottage. The nurses would kiss and cuddle us when they tucked us in to sleep at night. I don't ever remember feeling more safe than at that time. The children told me the foster mother had come out of her room the next morning to see if I was up. She told them she would get me on my return. But as fate would have it, she was moved and I didn't come in contact with her again.

Sports Day was held once a year. It was a big show day when we had to look our best for the outside visitors and relatives, to let them see how happy we all were and how lucky we were to be in such a Home. This was one of the days (like Christmas) when the girls were allowed to put their hair in crakes. This means you take a very small piece of hair at a time and curl it round a piece of rag and tied it round in a knot. Next morning (after a very sleepless night) you would take the rags off and there you were with crisp curls and there would be someone to comb out those tangles while you tried to fight back the tears.

Right from my very first day I think I was told I wasn't pretty. In fact, very ugly and this worried me a lot. I wouldn't face anyone, and trying to look pretty was very much against the rules. If you were caught looking in a mirror it was more than your life was worth. Being vain was one of the deadly sins. After a few Sports Days I found I wasn't ugly. The boys were looking at me with the come hither look. Of course that was all they were allowed anyway. But it made me feel better. As the ugly duckling would say, 'I'm a swan'. Leading up to Sports Day we would work very hard cleaning in every corner so on the day it looked as if we didn't work. It just appeared that way, for we were all so clean and tidy. No cooking was done so we didn't have to black-lead the cooking range. We were all given a lump of bread pudding for our dinner. I remember it well, with lumps of suet in it. We found it wasn't very good in the swimming races. It pulled you to the bottom of the water, but you were hungry so you ate it. It might be all you would get that day. Prizes for good work over the year were given out on Sports Day by the Board of Guardians. The prizes were mostly books but you felt very lucky if you were one of the chosen few. Swimming was one of my great outlets. How it worked was we would go swimming in our school time as a lesson. I learned to swim faster than anyone, but when it came to practice for swimming galas it meant asking the foster mother if she would let you off working duty for an hour in the evening. A great fear would come over me as I stood outside of her room trying to pluck up courage to knock on her door and ask, 'Please, may I go swimming?' The other girls used to say, 'Go on. She can't kill you'. (I wondered.) 'She can only say "No"'. Well, the first time I got my answer, 'Swimming, swimming, certainly not'. After that, the teacher wrote her a note, and told her I was a good swimmer and what an honour it would be for Mulberry Cottage if I came out top on Sports Day. Which, of course, I did. All the swimming team did so well, someone thought up the great idea that we could compete with the outside schools. This made us really practise very hard and we were all very excited and having a lot of fun, because somehow in the water you feel free. Then the bombshell for me. The order came through. No one could enter in any of the swimming competitions without a Birth Certificate. Of course, I wasn't the only one to be disappointed, but I was the top swimmer and the blow was hard to take.

Every evening, winter or summer, we would have to stay in one room to mend and patch all our clothing, knit all our black stockings when necessary. This was after we had done cleaning, scrubbing, polishing. To go out in the open air and play games was unheard of. If we had no mending or knitting to do, we were put on making mats with strips of material. They were called rag mats and mats with coloured wools. Knitting always had to be near at hand, at mealtime if you had finished your meal before the others the foster mother would say, 'Where is your knitting. Don't sit there idle. Satan finds mischief for idle hands to do'.

So there wasn't much time for fun or reading books. Though on Sundays Matron had what she called a library and if we were brave enough to say we had time to read a book (Sundays only) some did venture to the holy of holies but I can't ever remember doing so. At night time in the winter months, while we were knitting, sewing, mending, sometime the foster mother would read a book aloud to us, Charles Dickens mostly. I cried buckets for little Nell. How could they treat her so? Once a week the foster mother would inspect our darning and sewing. If the darns in our stockings were not up to her standards she would cut it out and make a much larger hole for us to mend. Once she cut the whole foot from my sock and told me to reknit it up before morning. I needed the stocking to wear for school next day. Unbeknown to anyone I sat up nearly all night sitting on the windowsill getting the light from the road outside, refooting my stocking. I didn't dare appear at breakfast without it.

She was ready for me, 'I didn't think you could get it done'.

Once a week the foster mother would have a half-day off and we always thought she might take a train to London. We felt like birds of the air just not to have her around. We did our work just the same but we could talk, laugh and have fun. At 9.30pm one of us would sit high on the window sill in the dormitory to listen for the train to tell us when she was at the station, and sure enough a few minutes later she would be coming round the corner towards the cottage where, of course, we would all be in bed fast asleep.

Once a month was what was called the Guardians' Day. When all the Board of Guardians would spend the day at the Homes, having meetings in the mornings in the big house called the Hollies where the head man of the Homes lived, a very big, frightening man, he terrified us all, and we would try to keep well away from him. My brother to this day feels cowed down by the violence he did to him in those days. Many more boys over the years must have carried their fear of him to the grave. He was in charge of the boys. Matron was in charge of the girls. We saw very little of her, making sure we kept our distance. The Guardians would have a very grand dinner put on for them at the Hollies, and when I was older (with other girls) we had to wait on table and clear away plates, which would have food left on them, much more food than we ever had, and we would get the plates in the kitchen and fight over the remains of the food. I remember on such an occasion, the food being much richer than we ever had, that I was sick all night, and the foster mother (who knew we ate the leftovers) said, 'Serve you right for being such a pig'. After this meal (which took about two hours) the Guardians would make their way round to inspect the cottages and as they entered we would have to stand at attention, and if you were spoken to, you had to drop a curtsey, with 'Yes, Sir', or 'Ma'm'. One day when they got around to Mulberry Cottage, we were having tea and as they entered we all stood, and waited for them to tell us when to sit down which they would say, 'You may sit down now, girls, and get on with your meal'. Which on this occasion was plum jam on our ration of bread. One of the guardians had their young daughter with them who looked at our bread and said something like, 'How revolting. It looks like Ronie' (which was a cleaner we polished the floors with.) It put me right off plum jam for ever. When the Guardians Day was over I think we all sighed a sigh of relief. 'Till next time for both children and staff.

School was quite a happy place, as long as we behaved ourselves and we tried. Being caned would upset us for the rest of the day, apart from having a very sore hand. As I got older I felt so ashamed in front of the whole class, it was so degrading. When I first went to school we had slates and slate pencils for writing adding up and taking away sums and then going in a higher class we used paper and pencil, followed by pen and ink and what a mess on my work that was, 'till we got used to it. Summer and winter we went into the playground to do drill. In the winter some of us would cry with the cold. So the teacher would let us put on our cloaks in twos and hold each other round the back. She called it playing two horses and we would run round the playground.

I didn't learn a lot at school. The classes were so large the teacher didn't seem to notice if you were not taking in what was going on. We didn't have school reports, nobody was that interested. I was very quick on mental arithmetic, which has held me in good stead in my working life. But as for reading aloud and spelling I sadly miss out. I never did have good handwriting. I should have gone to evening classes when I left the Homes but I was put in Domestic Service which only gave one half day off a week so that wasn't possible. Anyway I spent that half day off most of the time in bed I would get so tired working from early morning till late at night.

School holidays were not what we looked forward to, it was a time the foster mother said was for spring-cleaning and in the summer the month's holiday seemed endless. I seemed to spend so much time on punishment doing extra work or being put on my own to do the very dirty jobs. One summer holiday we did have a surprise. Some kind people paid for us to go to the seaside for a day. We went by train. Not being used to travelling I was sick all the way. But I was all right when we got there (Dovercourt, the seaside). We had lots of fun playing on the beach and paddling in the sea. Christmas holidays were shorter and being it got dark early, the working hours were less. We would help make Christmas

Puddings, we'd stone the raisins, chop the suet. We would have to sing while stoning the raisins so we couldn't eat any, not that we would dare.

One day that stands out at school was Armistice Day. For the first four years I was in the Institution the First World War was on. I don't remember much about it. We all seemed to be fighting our own private battles to keep alive. At school the older girls were calling out, 'The war is over!' and they were very happy about it. I wondered what difference it would make for us. Would everything be nice? But everything was the same. Every one had to attend the Armistice Service in the school hall and stand at attention through the service. Some of the lady teachers cried all the time, because their menfolk wouldn't be home from the war. Then a long list of old boys from the Home was read out as killed or missing. Come to think of them now, what a poor life they had. Then some of the brothers and sisters cried. That was a sad day for all with the boys' band playing on their trumpet the last part and in that great hall you could have heard a pin drop.

We were told to leave the hall in silence and think on our brave boys who had not come back from the war. I'm afraid it wasn't until World War II that I knew what this was all about. All I wanted to do was to put my arm around my friend who was six years old and crying so much. Her big brother still had not come home. In my childlike way I suppose I was saying he still might come back and see her and I hoped he would.

When I was twelve years old I knew all the ropes and how to keep out of trouble, what to do and what not to do. So I was quite surprised one morning after breakfast when the foster mother said to me, 'Matron wants to see you after school this afternoon. So make sure you are clean and tidy'. Now a command from matron invariably meant trouble or punishment. So all the girls looked at me with great pity, wondering what I had done wrong. Being that this was my very first command from Matron (I avoided her like the plague), I spent the day worrying about it. So at 4 o'clock, with some of the girls hiding behind trees, I walked up the path to Matron's house, waited a while, then rang the bell. One of the older girls came to the door and said, 'Oh yes, Matron is expecting you'. I waved to the girls hiding behind the trees, went in and the door was shut. We went along a hall and the girl knocked on the door where

Matron was. A voice said, 'Come in'. The girl said, 'Rose Harris to see you, Madam'. She said, 'Thank you, Mary', and Mary went out and shut the door.

Then Matron turned to me. 'Sit down, child. I have something very important to say to you. I have been approached by the Ladies' College at Eltham to have my permission if they could start a Girl Guide company in our Homes, and was wondering if you would be the leader and ask around, girls of your age, if this would be possible?' I didn't think I was hearing right. 'They need 12 girls altogether to start the company. They are coming Tuesday week, all being well, and will you meet at 7 to 8.30pm in the gymnasium?' I was thinking, 'Are we going to be allowed to enjoy ourselves? For one and a half hours in the evening with ladies from outside'. She must have noticed the look of glee and surprise on my face, for she smiled and said, 'That's all for now. Let me have the names as soon as possible'. I went down the path almost in a dream. The girls came out of their hiding places, saying, 'What have you done? What did she say?' I said, 'Let's go round behind the work shops' (where the boys did their boot mending and other jobs). As I unfolded the story their eyes opened wide and so did their mouths. The couldn't believe what I was saying. They all started talking at once, 'But Girl Guides do all sorts of exciting things, they hike and camp and they work at things they want to do' 'So', I shouted out, 'well, who wants to join?' And of course everybody did. So I soon made up 12 girls of the right age. Girl Guiding opened up a really bright, interesting world for us. We had a lot more free time because every time the College ladies wanted us to do something new they would ask Matron and she couldn't very well say, 'No', so we found ourselves working for all kinds of badges and as time went on we were learning more and more about the outside world.

We would have speakers in to talk to us. One evening we had a sea captain to give us a talk on the stars and at the end of the evening he said, 'I would like you to write down all I have been saying and bring it along with you next week'. Which, of course, we all did.

About a month later, I was told I had to go to the Hollies to appear before the Board of Guardians. I was more grown up now and I didn't fear the Board of Guardians so much. I was told that my essay on the stars after the talk of Captain Squires had been voted the best by the Astronomer Royal (at that time, F.W. Dyson). That was in

March of 1926. I was given a leather bound book of the classic, *Lorna Doone*, by R. D. Blackmore, which I still have to this day. It's still wonderful and a joy to have.

When I first went to school until I was about eight years old, primary school years, we were never allowed to drink anything between meals, not that there was anything apart from water. It didn't matter how hot the day, or how thirsty we were, we had to wait until meal time, breakfast and tea, when we had half a mug of milk and water, which wasn't allowed to be drunk 'till after we had eaten all our bread. As you can guess, even though we were hungry we found it difficult to do. Their excuse was to save us from wetting the beds. Now and again children did wet their beds, not because of the water they drank, but out of fear they might do it and the punishment they would get.

I remember the day when the foster mother went on holiday for a month and we had a relief foster mother and when one of the children was unwell and we all crowded around her to see what was wrong, the foster mother said to her, 'When did you last have a drink?' and we all looked at her, and said, 'We are not allowed drinks'. And she said, 'Of course you are. You can drink as much water as you like. Go and get some water for her'. We all flew to the cold water taps and drank our fill. How lovely it was. And every playtime at school we would spend it drinking water. There were far fewer wet beds after that. I think our bodies needed that water.

There were no inside toilets for children, only one which was used by the foster mother. The toilets and washroom were about twenty yards from the cottage. There were two toilets where, of course, most of the time we would have to queue. The washroom and toilets were very cold in winter and almost always frozen up. The washroom was also where we prepared all the vegetables, potatoes and swedes in freezing cold water, which was more like a punishment job. I once had to clean six pairs of muddy boots in the washroom, on a very snowy afternoon. No heat in there whatsoever. I was crying with the cold and couldn't hold the boot brushes. My hands were numb with the cold. We all had chilblains on hands and feet. I had them on the back of my heels. They would crack and be very painful. We all shed tears in the cold weather.

The warmest place to be, of course, was bed, and sometimes it was hard to get up in the morning. The foster mother's bedroom was in between the dormitories, with windows. She would peer out on us. Oh dear, that face at the window! In the wintertime we would have a bit more time to get out of bed before she saw us. Her light would go on and one of us that might be awake would call, 'Come on. She's up. She be out in a minute', and we would all move very fast for we never knew what punishment she would think of next.

Of course, a few of the children ran away. I would think how brave they were, and how did they do it? Everywhere was so fenced in and high gates locked but they still seemed to manage it. Some would get caught quite quickly and come back in tears. Others would make it; but we would never know what happened to them. It was no good me running away. Where would I go? I had no one to run to. When we were in our teens, sometimes on a Saturday afternoon near Christmas, we were allowed to go out of the houses to see the shops in the High Street. Now this was very queer for us to go outside those locked gates. Of course we had to keep together, but to us it was forbidden ground for so long it was almost impossible to know what to do with such freedom. It was like breathing different air. We got to a grocer's shop. We must have looked very hungry because the man came out and gave us all a penny bag of broken biscuits. We ate every crumb before we returned. We saw all the shops lit up for Christmas. We didn't have any money to spend, of course, but to breathe the High Street air did us all a power of good. I had never seen the High Street shops before. I expect, to the outsider, we looked proper waifs and strays, which, of course, was what we were.

I enjoyed that afternoon looking back. And yet we were brought up to work, not to enjoy life. That was a sin. If we were not working, we would be asked, 'Why are you wasting your time?' It wasn't until I was in the Army, I had just finished my eight-hour shift, someone shouted out, 'Are you going to the dance? Enjoy yourself!' Yes, enjoy myself. For the first time I didn't feel guilty.

Sex was never mentioned. One would find out a bit about oneself when the frightful day came for the first menstrual. I thought I was dying. The foster mother just said, 'Go and clean yourself up and wash your clothes', and she sent me to one of the older girls to tell me all about it. Or rather what she knew. She gave me some calico squares to fold up and wear with a bit of tape. 'You have to change often and wash the squares straight away and don't leave anything where other girls will see them'. I felt so unclean. She said, 'Don't worry. It only lasts a week and comes once a month. It just means you have grown up now'. I didn't want to grow up if this is what it meant. That was all I was told about sex. When I left the Homes to go into service, I was given 24 of these calico squares. I managed to wash them without the mistress seeing them but couldn't think of how I was going to get them dry, so I put them about the bedroom. My bedroom door was open when she passed the door and she was horrified. 'What's all this?' she said. 'I've got to dry them somewhere', I said. She just said, 'Oh dear. I will give you extra money to buy what you need from the chemist'. And she gave me the money, one shilling, and told me what to ask for. I was so grateful to be comfortable and not wear calico squares which rubbed so and made the skin raw. So, of course, what I knew about sex was very hush-hush.

We were all in the same boat. Neither teachers nor anyone in charge told us anything. My brother was sent to Canada (with many other boys) and I know they learned the hard way, as most of us must have done. It doesn't bear thinking about how many young people suffered by just not knowing the facts of life.

A few months before I left the Homes rumours were going round that there were going to be great changes in the way the Homes were run and sure enough when I returned for a visit to see some of my friends I had left I could hardly believe my eyes. The great iron gates had gone. The Homes had been taken over by the London County Council. What a change. The children were having beans on toast for tea. They said they were having lovely food. They could have as much as they wanted. They wore pretty clothes and for school they wore white blouses and skirts and panama hats, just like the outside schools. That was the fashion those days. Oh, how I would have loved a Panama hat!

Daily women were employed to do all the heavy work. The back gardens were dug up and made into playing areas. Bats and balls and skipping ropes appeared. Boys were now able to play football and the girls tennis. And they could go swimming when they wanted to. Now there were no gates to stop them, they could go for walks outside. There were what we call open days; nice teas would be laid on for children's families and visitors. That wasn't all. Brothers and sisters were living in the same cottages, like real families. Alas, this change was too late for me, but for the children still left in the Homes it was a much brighter future. I envied them.

'Do not speak unless you are spoken to', the Matron had warned. Six of us sat on a form in Matron's office to be viewed by our prospective employer. It was a hot day in July. The door was opened with great ceremony. We all stood, and in walked Matron with a very large pregnant woman, although I did not realise at the time she was pregnant, as sex education was never taught and I knew very little then. Matron walked down the line telling the lady about each one of us in turn, and what we were capable of doing. Needless to say the Lady was looking for a Domestic Servant.

We were all used to scrubbing floors, polishing and cleaning and black-leading grates. In the last year we were taught basic cookery and spent one day a week in the laundry, learning how to wash, starch and iron – with heavy flat irons, which were heated on a red-hot stove in the ironing room. Yes, I'd learned a lot, and I knew it all. I was sixteen years old, and looked forward to going out in the world. What a shock I had in store. It hadn't occurred to me that one day I might be on my own. In the Institution I had my friends. We had learned, worked and played together for over thirteen years. Soon, I'd have no one.

'You're very lucky, Rose. You have been chosen'. Everything moved very quickly. I was taken to a clothing store in town and fitted out with two of everything. These clothes were put into a tin trunk. How I got to this place of work, I do not remember. The Assistant Matron had brought me, and in saying 'Goodbye', reminded me yet again how lucky I was to have been chosen. Then she was gone, and I was alone. I hadn't felt so alone since my mother had left me at the Institution all those many years before. But this time I didn't cry. I went to my bedroom. It was in the attic. In the room was a bed, a wooden chair and a table with a basin and water jug, a rail to hang my clothes on and in the corner my tin trunk. I remember looking out of the window and seeing buses and cars going by, and a newsboy on the corner calling out to buy his papers. So much noise. This was indeed a new world!

In August 1992, Carol, my niece and her husband, Alan, having not visited England before, asked to visit the Hollies where both her dad and I had been as children. At that time the Hollies was being refurbished and being converted into private accommodation.

I guided them on a day trip – Carol's dad George, had been a talented lad and had sung in the church choir and been in the school orchestra. Carol wanted to see the church were he had sung and the school he had attended. All was much as she had imagined minus the gates and fences, even the old cinder path remained minus the grains of cinders imbedded in George's hands from childhood.

We all wandered along the road to what used to be Mulberry cottage, where I had been accommodated – now a private residence, after stopping for a photograph we went onto Limes cottage were my brother George had spent eight years of his life along with 50 other boys. The Limes had been totally refurbished, having been converted to six luxury apartments. The only remaining emblems from the past being two fireplaces and the staircase under which George had spent time standing in his nightshirt and bare feet with hands on head for punishment, Carol had shown her dad the photo on her return to Canada, it brought a smile but he never wanted a copy as it brought many bad memories!

The three of us carried on with their tour, visiting the pool – then ice cold, now luxuriously heated and newly refurbished gym. The headmaster's house was originally called the Hollies that had yet to be modernized and was in a state of dilapidation, but I found the old path, round the back of the house still there where I had walked some sixty-five years before!

Rose's daughter Georgina Peacock completed her mother's story:

As parents we want the best for our children, so I wonder how bad life must have been for my grandparents to put my mother and her brother into the Poor Law Institute Home at Sidcup – for they surely thought their children had a better chance inside the Home, than out.

The stories in this book are very familiar to me, my mother having told them many times. We have laughed and cried, and I marvel at how she survived. I know the scars must have been very deep, for as a child I remember her sleep walking and being woken by her screams in the night. Yet the love of our Lord Jesus overcomes all things. Her Christian faith lifted her above bitterness, hatred and resentment. I really had the best mum in all the world.

When Rose left The Hollies, she was on her own – in her first job she worked from 5am till 11pm. She had Thursday afternoon off and Sunday evening to go to church she was paid five shillings a week (25p). She was in service for the next 12 years, at first she 'lived in', her life was very hard, but it was all she knew. She enjoyed the fellowship of the local church and joined the guide pack. The leaders of the pack would become life-long friends and were horrified when after a few years Rose decided to get some 'rooms'. Rose on the other hand enjoyed this new freedom; she only had to work from 7am to 7pm for five days and 7am till 1pm on Saturday.

It was on a Saturday afternoon whilst walking on Blackheath with a friend that they were attracted to the Army enlistment tent, more interested in the soldiers than the army! However two days before war was declared she received her call up papers telling her to report the next morning, had she done so, she would have automatically been given the rank of Sergeant, but she had to tell her employer (who was furious). It was Monday when Rose found herself travelling to Sevenoaks in a van with a soldier either side, she said she was never so embarrassed or close to a man before! For the next seven years Rose was in the Auxiliary Training Service catering, her records show commendations for catering excellence, she eventually became Sergeant, her final posting was Bletchley Park, at an institution whose work was vital to the war effort.

Rose took the war in her stride, her rooms and later her flat was bombed, she did not like air raids and only slept in a shelter once and would never leave the theatre or cinema if an air raid was on. In 1941 she met my dad and was married in 1942. After the war she became a Guide Captain and would often entertain the Girl Guides from The Hollies at Christmas or tea in the summer.

Money was scarce and in 1952 Rose went to work in a School kitchen. She started as a cleaner and worked up to be the controller of 2000 meals a day. She retired in 1973. She was a devout member other local church and became a Samaritan. In 1975 my dad became ill with Alzheimer's and she nursed him for nine years up to the last six months of his life. At the same time she would be looking after her grandchildren, first Neil, then Ross and later Hannah, whilst I worked. Rose kept in touch with her brother all her life. I remember long after the war he sent food hampers from Canada and she would knit gloves and scarves for his children – they never saw their mother again. Uncle George yearned to meet her, but Rose was resigned to the fact that she wasn't wanted – although having gone through the workhouse records now I wonder, probably neither would have survived had they not gone to The Hollies.

Rose died in October 1994; in her own words she only had cancer nothing to concern anyone about. She lived her life as best she could and left her destiny up to the Almighty!

I dedicate my mother's memory to her Grandchildren Neil, Ross and Hannah.

Note: You can read more about Rose's life on
www.umilta.Net/rose.html
and on
www.umilta.Net/rose2.html.

HARRY A. READ 1917–1928

My father died of T.B. (Rapid Consumption) at the age of 32 years. He left five children and my mother had to go to the relieving officer to ask for help to bring up her five children.

She sold pieces of furniture for three months in an attempt to provide for us but did not earn enough money. Four of the children were sent to Sidcup Homes not through neglect but simply because there was no state allowance to cover the family. My mother obtained a job as a cleaner at the Greenwich Union Workhouse in London, but the income was again too small to enable her to regain the children and look after them. We had schooling and some job training at the Sidcup Homes, then when able to go to work returned home to our mother.

The parting of the small boy from his mother was heart rending and the anguish could be seen on the mother's face the child sobbing his heart out as his mother walked away with tears in her eyes. That boy was myself, Harry A. Read, age six years. I shall try to explain the upbringing and the other children whose misfortune it was to end up in the Homes.

A very worried Lady with a small child was to be seen walking along Burnt Oak Lane, Sidcup, Kent. She was aware of what was ahead of her having experienced a similar situation the previous year. They both arrived at big wrought iron gates. Pulled a well-polished bell knob and a bell could be heard in the vicinity of a cottage known as the 'Pro'. (Probation wards)

Still sobbing I was taken into the cottage and placed in a room spotlessly clean, sparsely furnished and well scrubbed table in the centre of the room flanked by two well scrubbed forms, there was nothing else in the room to interest me or any other child.

After what seemed hours a man came into the room, draped a cloth round me and began to cut my hair off with hair clippers. When he had completed his work, in spite of my struggles, a lady came in and began to comb my hair with a 'tooth close', when she had finished she took me to the bathroom. I was then stripped, bathed and given a nightshirt and put to bed, I can't recall having anything to eat or whether I refused to eat.

I was in the pro for about a week and then taken to one of the girls' cottages which housed 20 to 25 girls and small boys, in charge was a middle aged lady and one of the senior girls acted an her assistant. Life in the cottage was not hard but strict discipline was enforced and any disobedience was severely dealt with. I must admit I rebelled against discipline and was punished for my behaviour, put to bed without my tea or deprived of my play by being made to stand in the cottage hall for an hour.

On a Saturday of each month was visiting day. My mother came to see me and in addition I was to see my brother Fred for the first time in over a year and was housed in the Firs, one of large houses, over the other side of the Home. Mother would bring us sweets, fruit and give us some money to spend. The visit only lasted about an hour and it was dreadful to see all the parents leaving their children behind, many of them in tears including me. Although my brother did his best to console me.

Between the girls' cottages, which were all named after trees, was the boiler house, baker house, laundry, swimming baths and the gymnasium. Beyond this was a ploughed field known as the '440' (yards), there were four large buildings, the Beeches, Firs, Limes and Oaks.

The routine of the house was practically the same every day except Saturday and Sunday: up at 7am, strip your bed, get dressed, go downstairs and wash. As you file out the washroom the foster father would inspect your nails, ears, look for any tide mark and your teeth and if you had a defect on any of these you had to completely wash again, that would mean a loss of playtime. Then upstairs make your bed and if you had not made it properly the lady helper would strip the bed and you had to do it all over again.

It was not so easy for the boys. A few of the older boys, about six of them had to be up at 6.30am. They stripped their beds went down into the kitchen to black-lead the kitchen range. It was of six feet in length, rub up the fender with emery paper and clean out two large ovens, clean the fire gate, relay the fire and light it and hope that it burns up or else.

While two boys were engaged on the above work, another two boys had to carry all the breakfast things into the dining room, lay the tables and prepare the staff tables, meantime two other boys would sweep out the room and polish the floor. At the conclusion of this work all the other boys are lining up ready to march in the dining room for their breakfast. Breakfast consisted of two slices of bread and treacle, and a gritty mug of cocoa. No larking about was allowed during meals. I received a clout in the ear one day, which finally resulted in having to go to hospital for a mastoid in the right ear. The eardrum had shattered. I was not aware that the clout was the cause of the mastoid late until late in life.

Punishment could be in the shape of standing in the hall whilst every child was at play. School was about half a mile from the houses and you were marched all the way until you reached about 400 yards from the school. Then you were on your own; the playground was divided by a fence. Fortunately you were able to talk to your sisters through the fence. The boys used to say to them, 'see that crowd over there' it's your brother Harry again fighting. Yes, I was nearly always fighting. I just could not stand tolerate any one taking the micky out of my voice impediment. More often than not, I used to get the worst of it, but they used to think twice before micky taking again. Yes, my sisters Mary and Emily arrived about 18 months after me. I went home one day with a lovely shiny black eye. The foster father said, 'Read, you've been fighting again, wait for me outside my study'. I had no idea what was coming, when he came I followed him to his study, he got out his cane and I had six of the best, three on each hand. But it didn't deter me from defending my principles.

We all filed into dinner. Have you ever been faced with yellow fat on your plate? We often had it and we were not allowed to leave the table until we had eaten the horrible muck, apart from that the dinner was not too unreasonable. After dinner we made our own way back to school, on the way we did what all boys do, play around. I remember that just about a hundred yards from the school there used to be a large oak tree and regularly up in the branches was a big white Owl. I think the old devil used to know when we were coming and was tempting us to climb up the tree after him.

On our return to the house we were allowed to go to the playing fields to play cricket, football or whatever. But we had to be back at the house by 5.30pm with clean boots that had to be put out for inspection after you had put your slippers on, then to wash ready for tea. We all lined up in the hall. Then the foster father called out the boys numbers who had not cleaned their boots to his satisfaction, the poor little devils had to clean their boots after they had tea, losing some of their playtime. Tea consisted of two slices of bread and jam with a cup of tea, you could if you were lucky if you had eaten your first two slices have another.

After play it was time for bed the small boys went to bed at 7pm and the older at 7.30pm, there were six bottom 10, 8 and 7, of the bedrooms had extras beds at times. When the foster father and his wife were off duty we used to have pillow fights. Top 10 versus bottom 10 and so on. The small boys were detailed to keep their eyes open in case one of the ladies came up.

Before I mention Saturday and Sunday, I feel that I should explain an incident that occurred around about 12pm. I was the fortunate boy, all of us had an attack of food poisoning. It appears that we all made a rush for the toilets, (there were only two available), I won't go into the sordid details, in the morning the foster father and his wife were rushing around with cane. Many of the boys were unable to retain themselves so we all had to line up in our night-shirts in the hall. There was no doubt the foster father was flaming mad, he caned quite a number of boys without any regard of the embarrassment to the boys. After all was cleaned up, we had our meal and were marched off to school on the way one of the boys, who had been severely punished fainted. The bandmaster who was always posted where the boys dispersed went to attend to the boy. He was told by the boy and the other boys what had happened, the bandmaster went off to see the foster father and all the boys followed him, including boys from the other houses. On the arrival to Firs he met the foster father and there were some angry words exchanged. As he left the boys were picking up lumps of turf and throwing them at the foster father. But it didn't stop there, they began to hit him with anything they could get hold of with the result he became severely injured and just about managed to reach the house before matters got even worse. Finally he had to attend hospital. The incident became known as the 'Air Raid on China'.

Saturday was the cleaning up day, all the bedrooms were to be sweep out and polished, the same with the stairs, the hall to be scrubbed. The floors were tiled with red tiles, kitchen floors and tables scrubbed. In fact, everything that needed cleaning was cleaned, including all the brass work, knives, forks and spoons. It was approximately 10.30am before we were allowed to go out to play. In the afternoon a cricket or football match was arranged between

The Firs, The Limes and The Oaks houses. We were allowed to stay up another half-hour on Saturdays.

Sunday we had a half-hour lay in. Breakfast we had a boiled egg, two slices of bread, followed with a slice of bread and marmalade. We then had to dress in our best suits ready for church. There was no church in the home so a priest was brought in the conduct the service. The service was ridiculous, we had a very old priest, who was shaking with age and boys and girls used to laugh and joke, at times there was complete disorder. A number of boys went to Lamorbey Church, amongst them was my brother Fred.

Dinner was better than the week day dinners and there was plenty of it. For sweets we had Yorkshire pudding with jam. After dinner boys had an half hour play then we were taken for a walk to places like Avery Hill, Falcon Wood (they were woods in those days), Blackfen to name but a few.

I conclude this by stating the Homes no doubt treated us right despite the discipline, which to my mind was essential to us all and it is a great pity that so many children had to be separated from their parents.

Note: Harry Read was born in 1911 and taken into care with three of his siblings. Mrs Read obtained a job as a cleaner at the Greenwich Union Workhouse but this was too low-paid a job to allow her to bring her children home. Harry refers in his account to 'my voice impediment': he was born with a hare lip and cleft palate on which he had operations in later life. Harry was a Labour councillor for Greenwich Metropolitan Borough then the London Borough of Greenwich from 1957-1978. He stated that the seeds of his socialist beliefs were sown through the terrible distress he and his family experienced when they had to be parted after the tragic death of his father. The system did not allow for emotions, he stated. When he became a governor and a former governor at Goldie Leigh Home by a fluke he discovered that his mastoid was caused by a blow he had received at the Sidcup Homes.

KATHLEEN WILKINS 1920-1927

When my mother died my father was left with six children. My younger brother was two and was looked after by my father and an aunt who lived in the same house. My elder sister went to live with another aunt. So my three brothers and I went to the Homes. Many people looked on us as paupers but my father paid for us, I have some of the receipts.

I was very happy at the Home and school. Two sisters were house-mothers in Olive and Chestnut. I lived in Olive Cottage. In the morning the eldest had to get up and clean the range, the foster mother would light the stove so we could have breakfast. The food was good but always the same menu, porridge, different stews and puddings with prunes, but the foster mother tried to give us a treat sometimes, when she had some eggs to spare she would make a sponge cake for tea especially if it was one of the children's birthday.

I remember one Christmas the students from Avery Hill College invited us to tea. They asked us what fancy dress we would like. I went as Miss Muffet and a little boy was the spider. My brothers were not very happy at the Homes, although they were good at cricket and swimming. When sports day came, parents were allowed to bring friends with them; my brothers won medals at swimming. I have one as keepsake.

One day my brothers decided to escape, they managed to get to Woolwich and caught the ferry, which they thought would take them abroad, sadly, they were returned to the Sidcup Homes. When my father re-married there were only my brother and I still left at the Homes, we were supposed to be collected but again sadly, we were left there. It was not until the following year my father was able to collect us and take us really home.

My brother and I had been allowed to enter an exam which enabled us to go to Greenwich Central School, although by that time I was living with my father.

The bond between my foster mother and myself was great. When I left the Homes she would meet me from school on her days off and we would spend a couple of hours together. When I was sixteen we went on holiday to Peacehaven, sadly the afternoon before leaving she was knocked down by a lorry while crossing the road. I was devastated. However, my father being out of work I had to work, happily I met a boy there who became my husband in 1940.

CATHERINE ELIZABETH HAZELWOOD (née Gomall) 1929
I was born on 16 July 1916, in Southwark, London, England. My father was forty-nine years of age when I arrived on the scene, I was an only child. In 1927, when I was eleven years old my mother died of pneumonia. I had been to the hospital on that last day to see her but I had no idea that she was dying. Her last words to me were 'Be a good girl for your father' and I promised her I would, never realizing that she was not going to get better. I left her and went outside in the corridor to tell my father that mother was talking to me and was getting better. He went in to see her next and then we left the hospital together, neither of us realizing that we had spoken our last words to her. We had not long been home before a policeman knocked at the door and told us that my mother had died.

My father was then 60 years of age. He was so shocked at the loss of his wife he felt he was unable to bring me up on his own. That very night Dad made an instant decision to leave our flat. I packed a few things and took my favourite doll and a little tin box with some letters in it, and my father and I went to my Aunt Emily's house. She was Mrs John Ward, my aunt and Dad's sister. She lived on Orkney Street, Battersea. He asked her to look after me for a few weeks until he could make arrangements for me. I never saw my own home again. I had nothing left of my mother's. Not a thing. My father was so distraught he gave everything away, including my toys and he moved out and went to his workshop. He was a firewood cutter. He was extremely deaf as a result of almost thirty years in the army and it was so difficult to communicate with him. We said very little to each other about Mother's death because of his disability. I really missed her because we had been so chose. She used to sing Irish folk songs to me. I have never found an Irish relative in my family background so I presume she just liked the music.

My Aunt Emily, to whom I had been taken, was very kind to me and I stayed with her for a few weeks. However, her brother-in-law, whose plumbing supply shop was underneath their flat, was a little strange in his behaviour, and he had a violent temper. My father was not happy that I was living there with the brother-in-law so close, and he took me away from there after a few weeks. I wished I could have stayed with Aunt Emily longer because I liked her very much, but indeed I was afraid of her brother-in-law Percy.

My father decided to move me closer to his workshop and to the small flat he took which was close to it. He paid a lady who lived nearby on the Borough High Street to look after me. He gave her nearly all his money to look after me, but it seemed that most of the money went on her children instead. I did not stay long with her but went to live in Deptford with the family of a fireman and his wife, Harold and Kate Hyde. They had just lost their little girl to diphtheria, and they were happy to take me in. I enjoyed living with them but it was not to be, and after six months there, Mr Hyde was offered a job in Mombasa, East Africa. They wanted to take me with them but my father wouldn't let me go because he thought he would never see me again. With the Hydes arranging to leave England I was on the move again.

Mr and Mrs Hyde took me to the Greenwich Board of Guardians and arrangements were made then to take me to their children's home in Sidcup, Kent. I had no idea that my father was not aware that I was being sent there. So, in early 1929, I went there in a private car with a nurse and I remember clearly the day we drove through the big wrought iron gates for the first time. I was delivered to the Lodge where the gatekeeper showed us the way to the Matron's quarters in the house called The Hollies.

All of the children in that school were housed in semi-detached cottages. They were very nice inside. I was taken to 'Poplar Cottage'. Upstairs in each cottage there were two dormitories which housed six children ranging in age from six to twelve years. A separate room housed two older girls whose ages were 13 and 14, and then the nurses had their own private rooms.

At the bottom of each child's bed there was a big box which contained two sets of clothes and this we were given plus the set we were wearing. The box contained underwear, shoes, stockings, and a dress. A set of towels were also in the box. The girls wore a gym slip. The school colours were grey and white. We had a grey velour hat and a warm grey coat. The initials GDCH (Greenwich and Deptford Children's Homes) were on the hat band. The stockings were black and we wore black lace-up boots.

The ground floor of each cottage had a dining room which seated everyone at the table at the same time including the nurse. There were fifteen of us that all sat down to meals together. The food was quite good. I didn't always like what we were served but we had eat it. Breakfast consisted of porridge or toast, and tea. Our main meal was mid-day. Sometimes it was stew and dumplings and other times it was fish, peas and carrots and boiled potatoes. I didn't like the Swedes (turnips) they served but I had to eat those too. High tea consisted of sometimes an egg, or cheese, bread and jam and tea. Occasionally a piece of cake was served. I don't remember anyone ever celebrating a birthday and having a cake when I was there.

After I had been there for two weeks it was visiting day which occurred once a month. Visitors were allowed for two hours between 2 and 4pm a month. I looked forward to my father's first visit there to see me. I was very disappointed when he didn't appear. Another month went by and I still didn't see him. I was very upset and cried a lot. I didn't know why he hadn't come to visit. Later I found out that I had been put in there without his consent or knowledge. I was worrying about him and he thought I was still living with the Hyde Family where he knew I was happy.

In The Hollies, the days were long and tiring. I got up at 7 o'clock in the morning. The older children had to get the younger ones ready for school. We had our breakfast during which time I had to help feed the little ones and cut up their food for them. After breakfast, we all walked down the drive across the green to the school which was enclosed in the grounds. After school we had chores to do. I had to clean 14 pairs of boots before I could have my tea. Very often there was little or nothing left for me by the time I had finished. After I had had my tea (if there was any left) I had to then go and help bath and dry the smaller children and get them ready for bed.

On Saturdays when there was no school, we had to go out to the back yard, and work in the laundry room for each cottage. We were taught how to do laundry and ironing. It was bitter cold in there in the winter time. Wringing out wet clothes in the cold weather was awful. I got very bad chaps on my hands and the nurse put glycerin on them. In the school there were also some children from outside but they were kept in a separate area away from us, so that we would not catch any diseases from them.

The children also had to do gardening there. The girls put plants in the flower beds, weeded and raked leaves. The older boys did the heavy digging in the gardens. I had to do my share of gardening too. However, I was so tired from cleaning all the boots in the cold porch every day, and getting thinner from lack of food at night when there was little or none left after all the other children had eaten theirs, that I became very depressed. The monotony of the same routine every day and the sadness I felt began to take its toll on me. I still had not seen my father.

I felt very deprived of love and affection in that school. It is hard to live in a place like that when you have lived in your own home with your parents. As I had been an only child and had my parents around me, it was very difficult to adjust to being in an institution.

I made plans to escape. I told the two older girls that I was going to run away. They asked me to find their parents and tell them how unhappy they were too. I planned to go back to Deptford to the Hydes because I knew they had not yet gone to Mombasa but were due to leave at any time. I had no money for streetcar fare so the two older girls very kindly loaned me some.

May 3rd 1929 will remain in my memory forever, as the night I ran away from the school. I was twelve years old. I chose to make good my escape on a Friday evening because I knew that our nurse was having the night off and she wouldn't be there at bedtime. I knew that the other nurse would drop in from next door to ensure that we were all in bed at night.

I waited until all the children including myself were all in bed and the nurse had been in to check on us. After she had gone, I got out of bed and took my clothes out of the box at the bottom of the bed, and rolled them up and put them in the bed to make it look as if I was in it. The little girl in the next bed watched me in amazement while I 'made up the bed'. I put my finger to my lips to indicate to her that she was not to say anything. Her name was Patricia Garcia. She was six years of age. She used to cry a lot and missed her mother. When they found I was missing, the school authorities questioned Patricia but she never told them she had seen me leave. (I wonder what happened to that little girl.)

I waited for a while and then tiptoed down the stairs carrying my hat and coat and shoes. One of the older girls let me out, wishing me good luck and asking me to go and see their mothers and fathers to tell them they didn't like it in there either. I told the girls not to lock the door after me so that it would look as if I went out by myself, thereby not getting anyone else into trouble.

I put my hat, coat and shoes on outside and with my little tin box which contained all my little treasures and letters, I prepared to run away. In order to get out of the area, I had to pass The Hollies where the matron lived, and so I went around the house to the bushes outside and hid there. As I was hiding there in the bushes, I heard the boys in the band and the band master, Mr Bonner, coming along the drive. I knew they would ask me why I was outside if they saw me, so I remained hidden until they had gone by. Then I had to crawl on my stomach across the grass. The Lodge door was open, and the lights were shining across the field. I knew they would see me if I stood up and ran across there. I crawled down as far as the fence which led to the Day School and I climbed over the fence into the school yard. From there I walked down to the bottom of the school yard and into the lane. The lane led to the High Street. I was frightened someone returning to the home would recognize me because I was wearing the school uniform. I took off my hat; to me it was less obvious that I belonged to the school.

In one of the shop doorways I left my little tin box containing all my treasures. Fortunately for me, the shop keeper when he opened the door the next morning found it and returned the tin to the school for me. I caught a bus on the Sidcup High Street which was going to the Bricklayer's Arms on the Old Kent Road which was the end of the line for that bus. I had to get on another bus from there. I sat there as we rode along, wishing I was one of the other people on that bus instead of me. I was so alone and afraid. I got off at the Bricklayer's Arms and unfortunately had no more money left for another bus fare. I still had to get to Evelyn Street, Deptford, to go the Hyde family. They had no idea I was coming.

I waited outside The Bricklayer's Arms until I saw an elderly lady coming along who looked kind. I took a chance and told her I had run away from the school and asked her if she could give me some money for the bus fare so that I could get to see Mr and Mrs Hyde at Deptford. She gave me tuppence and said she hoped I knew what I was doing. I think that was probably all the money she had with her. I got on the next bus and eventually got to Mr and Mrs Hyde's house on Evelyn Street at Deptford.

I knocked on their door, and by this time it was very late in the evening. Mrs Hyde opened the door and when she saw me standing there she was so surprised, and said, 'Oh Katy! What are you doing here?' I told her I had run away from the school. Her husband joined her at the door and the look of dismay on their faces was evident. She said 'Oh my! We can't keep you here tonight. We are leaving on the ship in the morning'. I looked behind her in the hall and could see all the trunks lined up against the wall.

Mr and Mrs Hyde called a taxi and they went with me to the Board of Guardians. By then it was very late at night. We saw the man on duty and he told me he had a son my age. I think he felt sorry for me. He was going to keep me there for the night, but then at the last minute he decided to send me to the Institution called The Greenwich Work House. Before we left for the Work House, he phoned the school to tell them I had 'escaped', and they were very surprised. They didn't even know I was missing. They weren't very happy. I was very worried because I didn't know what they were going to do to me as a punishment for running away.

I went by car with the Hydes to the Workhouse and they left me there. The man from the Board of Guardians went with us too. When I arrived at the Greenwich Workhouse, I was taken to a section full of elderly ladies. One of the women gave up her bed for me, and they put her somewhere else for the night. The bed was in an alcove. I remember the lady stripping off the sheets and putting clean ones on it for me. The other ladies in there kept asking me why I was there. They commented on my clothes and how nice they were and asked me why did I want to run away from a place that dressed me so well? I had had no food for many hours so a glass of milk was brought for me.

The next morning a chauffeur-driven car arrived to take me back to the school. A nurse dressed in a blue uniform went with me. The chauffeur whistled all the way to the school, and I can remember the song now – it was 'Laugh, Clown Laugh'. I kept thinking he wouldn't whistle that if he was in my position.

When I arrived back at the Greenwich school, I was taken to the Lodge and then they advised the Matron that I had arrived. I had never met the Matron and I was expecting I suppose, a large woman with a loud manner, (possibly someone similar to a character out of a Charles Dickens' book). I was very surprised to find she was small in stature with a nice face, and very pleasant to me. She said 'Catherine, why did you run away? Were we unkind to you?' I had to explain to her that they had not been unkind to me, but that I had been put in there so quickly and didn't know why my father had not been to see me. I told her I was very unhappy. I explained that I had no time to have my tea at night because I had to clean 14 pairs of boots right after school. I described how I had to scour the boots of any mud before I could start to polish them, and then the kind of polish I used was the sort that the army used. You put it on dry, spit on it and then rubbed it into the leather. It took me a long, long time to get the boots cleaned and shiny and polished properly, and by then there was no food left for me. Also, I had to help bath the small children before I went to bed. I told her I was too afraid to complain. In fact I told her everything. I sat there with her and cried.

The Matron listened to me. She wasn't angry with me. She was very nice. She said I should have told the nurse in the cottage that I was not getting any food to eat after school. Furthermore, she said I should have told them how unhappy I was. She said her job was to make sure the children were happy in the school, even though they had no parents there. I wondered how anyone could be happy in there with the routine that we had to live with each day.

Naturally, the other children were surprised to see me back so soon. It probably dashed any ideas any others might have had with regard to escape. My father was contacted and he came to see me a day or so later. The school must have sent someone to find him and tell him where I was. They didn't make me wait until the next visiting day. He explained that he didn't know that I was in there. He gave me the money to repay the girls for the bus fare I had borrowed from them.

The number of pairs of boots I had to clean was reduced in number and arrangements were made for me to eat first and clean the boots later. Things improved a little from there on.

A month later I left The Homes, and was taken to the Central London District School in Hanwell, Middlesex. It turned out that I had not lived in Greenwich with the Hyde family long enough to qualify to attend The Homes so I was transferred out of there. That was in relation to the Poor Law which stated that an individual had to have lived in that district for a certain length of time before the local council would help support them. If you did not meet those requirements you were physically taken back to the district from whence you came.

I never heard from Mr and Mrs Hyde again. I often pondered what my life would have been like if my father had given me permission to go to Mombasa with them. What happened to them I wonder?

The Central London District School in Hanwell became my home from July 1929 until 17 March, 1930. I liked it there. I had a lot of hard work to do like scrubbing corridors and other duties, but I worked hard at my studies and I earned a scholarship from that school. My name went on a plaque in that school as one of those who earned a scholarship.

From the Central London District School, I went to the London Borough Polytechnic for two years. It was the first Trade School for girls in London. Some of the subjects learned in there were dressmaking, tailoring, and the sciences. I decided to learn how to cook and be a Lady's companion. I had to take all the general subjects and passed with honours in all subjects including cookery.

While I was there I was very fortunate to become chosen as a Ward of Lady Helen Barlow who looked after the expense of my room and board and my clothes. The Polytechnic was not a live-in school. During the time I was there I was invited to her home for tea with some of the other girls in the small group that she sponsored. She was very kind to us and I felt very privileged to go her home in Wimpole Street, London. There were games organized for us when we went there and the treasure hunt led all through her house. Most of the rooms were open to us, and those that were off limits were marked as being so. Lady Barlow sat at the piano and played and sang to us. She had a very nice voice and I can recall she sang 'Cherry Ripe' and 'Strawberry Fair'.

I studied hard at the London Borough Polytechnic and passed, receiving my Diploma in Cookery. When I left there I then had to start working my way up from the bottom to eventually become a Cook or a Chef, which was my ambition at the time. Because of my good record (except for running away from The Hollies) and my good marks, I was fortunate in acquiring my first position, as Scullery Maid with the Guinness family of Lord Moyne, who lived at 10–11 Grosvenor Place, London. It was a beautiful house, several hundred years old and full of marvellous antiques and paintings. It was very close to Buckingham Palace, and when I was on the top floor I could look down into the Palace Gardens. Sometimes I saw King George V walking in there.

Starting work for the Guinness family was indeed an apprenticeship for me. They had 32 servants in that house. The Guinness family was very good to their staff and we certainly lacked for nothing in the way of good food. Employees were offered a glass of Guinness Stout every day if they were of legal age to drink. My working hours there were from six o'clock in the morning, to eight o'clock at night, with a three hour break after two pm. I had to wash and dry the plates and pots and pans. There was a huge rack on the wall in the kitchen in which I had to place all the plates after I had washed and dried them.

Because I was not very tall, I had to stand on a chair and clean the bottoms of the large saucepans which were on the high draining board. My job was to scrub the copper bottoms of the pots with sand and vinegar which was mixed with flour to make a paste. I developed a bad rash on my arms from the vinegar which ran down as I scrubbed the pots. (No rubber gloves in those days). Every night I had to peel potatoes for thirty two people. I had to soak them in cold water overnight so that they were ready for the next day's meals for the staff. I had two half days off a week. The night before my half day I had to peel enough potatoes for 64 people to cover the two days I wasn't there. I hated that job. I still hate peeling potatoes today.

I wasn't supposed to cook in those early days at the Guinness home; just do the Scullery Maid work. However, the Cook soon found out that I had done very well in cookery at the London Borough Polytechnic and that I could make very good sauces and prepare vegetables. She let me help her make the sauces (and she took the credit for it too). Lord Moyne was very fussy about his vegetables and he liked the way I prepared and cooked them, and eventually for the time I was there, I prepared and cooked all his vegetables for him.

We had to prepare huge dinners for banquets and balls, and sometimes the Duke and Duchess of York (later the Queen Mother) and other Royalty would attend. On those occasions, the Butler would allow the staff to go up to the dome and the gallery over the ballroom and watch through the glass skylights from above the chandeliers, the guests dancing far below. When I went there I noticed that there were two railings around the gallery. I was told that previously and just before I arrived there, only one railing had been in place. However, a young woman on the staff had leaned too far out over the railing and had fallen through the glass skylights and crashed onto the Ballroom floor. I was told it was an occasion when the Prince of Wales was there. The girl was very badly hurt and the Guinness family undertook to care for her financially for the rest of her life as she was unable to walk again. I was sad to read that Lord Moyne was assassinated in 1940 in mistake for someone else. He was a kind man and a good employer.

The staff was also allowed to go and have a look at the tables when they were set for a banquet. Outside caterers were brought in on those occasions to do the flowers, the table settings and the decorations. The tables were absolutely stunning as they sparkled with all the crystal and silver. The floral decorations were reflected in the mirrors on the walls. I loved to go around and read all the names of the guests at the place settings. They read like 'Who's Who'. I learned a lot of interesting things there which I will always remember.

I left the employ of the Guinness family when I developed rheumatism and could no longer stand on a cold, hard kitchen floor for long hours. I worked for Lady Hester Duncombe as her Lady's Companion for a while. It was exciting being with her and travelling to other country homes. However, it became very lonely for me. I was just eighteen at the time and yearned for the company of other young people. Lady Duncombe was very kind to me and sorry when I left her employ.

My days of cooking and working for the aristocracy came to an end when I married at the age of 23 and my husband learned what a good apple pie I could make. I do believe that children who have been in schools like The Homes (particularly girls) made good wives in those days because they were so grateful to have a husband who cared for them and looked after them, and with whom they could share affection. The latter is the one thing that is so necessary and yet is so void in any institutional setting.

JACK WHITEPOST 1911-1921

My story is peculiar. In the first place, I don't know where I was born. In the second place, I know nothing about my family. You've heard of foundlings? Where kids are abandoned on the streets and sent to the orphanage homes to be raised? Well that was my lot! I went there when I was three years old so I was just an infant. We had two probation [wards] where kids coming into the Home spent so much time in each place, be they boy or girl, to see they had no communicable diseases or things like that. They would spend maybe a month there and they would then go to one of the other cottages. That's where I grew up!

As long as you behaved yourself, you had no trouble. If you didn't, well you got the cane! Now the cane is far worst than a miserable little strap that never hurt anybody!

We had a big meadow right near the school. But we weren't allowed to cross that meadow. We had to walk all the way around. But I remember one afternoon, as many as 32 kids got the cane for cutting across that field. Just for that! If you got the cane, well they made you bend down and touch your toes, and pull your trousers good and tight, and they brought that cane down across your other end. And you felt it! And we had one teacher who made you bend down, touch your toes, and make you shove your head under the desk. When they brought down that cane, then you bob up and you'd hit the back of your head. So you got it coming and going! Those were rare cases but they did happen. It happened to me once, so I was no better than anybody else. As long as we behaved ourselves and lived by the rules, we were fine.

Cleanliness was one thing that was emphasised. We had to keep clean! First thing in the morning, last thing at night, and at least once a week, a good hot bath. Everything; clean clothes twice a week. We had to shine our own shoes every night, clean and shining for the next morning. We had two pairs of shoes. Our Sunday shoes we cleaned on Monday ready for the next Sunday. We had to do all these things ourselves and as got older, all these things that I had to do, as a kid, came in very handy. Even to this day, if my wife's away, I can cook up a meal without ant trouble at all! But if I had to, it's no problem. It's a wonderful education. I look at teachers that we had and I look back at that home now. And I have lovely memories.

It might sound to you that we had a hard life, but it wasn't. We accepted it and we were enjoying ourselves in our own way. We weren't allowed to read a newspaper and some of the words that we use today, that are accepted even, we'd have got the cane if we'd used them then. If I'd said something like that guy's a regular old bum, in England, I'd have got the cane. That's a swear word! Our parents would turn over in their graves if they heard the language of today. You can't criticize the young people. It's the age you live in. I know it's hard to make the young people understand. But they'll only get out of life just what they put into it.

We had special uniforms to wear and we were all dressed alike. A lot of the kids coming into the Home wouldn't take to it very easily and the first chance they got, they'd run away. The authorities would chase them no matter what part of England they went to and bring them back to the Home. Boys were punished with a birch across the bare back. The reason they got the birch was not for running away. The punishment was for stealing – just the clothes they were wearing. The clothes belonged to the Home not the children. That's the kind of discipline I grew up under.

We hadn't had time for hobbies. There were two lady assistants to see that we kept ourselves clean and tidy. But us children had to do all the work. We had to scrub the floors, make the beds and clean the windows. We had little or no time to play what we call hobbies. When you get home at half past four in the afternoon, then you started with this housework. We all grew our own vegetables and us children were out hoeing the fields. We had very little spare time!

If you weren't doing that after school, if you were in the band, which I was for three years, you headed to the band room for two hours of practice. Also I was fortunate enough to sing in the village choir out of the orphanage. We used to get paid eleven shillings every three months for singing. I used to get paid extra for singing at weddings and funerals. The funerals paid the best. We used to pray there'd be a lot of funerals. We'd get more money! The singing got us out of the orphanage home at least two nights a week for practice and practically all day Sunday. So it made a fairly good life for all, but as I say, as for hobbies, we had no time for them. We did a lot of walking out through the countryside, not alone, all controlled.

The first car I saw in England was a little sports car. That part was fine. But you take trucks! I remember they used to haul coal into the orphanage home by truck and it was steam driven! Can you imagine a truck being driven with that kind of power? 12 miles an hour was the speed! Now remember there was no such thing as radio, no television. Cars were few and far between.

During the First World War, I still can't reconcile why, when an air raid came came in the daytime, as they did periodically, they'd send us home from school. We had a mile and a half to run home with that thing going on up there! Silly, isn't it? Take in the First World War in the area where I lived, we had air raids that were done by German Zeppelins, you know, these lighter than aircraft blimps. I hope to never see that again!

We had our workshops. I started out to be a tailor, but I didn't like that, I went into the carpentry workshop and found I couldn't cut a board straight! Anyway, we had our own brass band and I played slide trombone.

I lived there until I was 13. Then the opportunity came one Sunday night after church for any boys who would like to go to Canada, to give their name. Well we didn't know anything about what we were going into, anyway 13 of us applied. Only 7 were accepted.

So after a while we went up to Liverpool to a holding home there for a matter of about two months till we got our medicals and outfitted with our clothing. Then on 22 July, 1921, we boarded a ship to come to Canada. In those days in the home were the beginning and the end of my schooling. According to the law then, we had to go to school in Canada for the first three months of the winter, for three months during the first winter we were here. All the grades were taught in this one room by one teacher.

I'll tell you how I found life when I first came to Canada. I was placed on this farm over at Peter's Corners which is about fifty miles from where we are now in Streetsville. It's between Dundas and Galt, near Cambridge. I was on that farm with a husband, his wife and their little boy, Lyle, not two years old that time. I was about thirteen. That little lad and I more or less grew up together, so that, to this day, we're still in contact. He's the closest person I even had to a brother and he says the same about me. He was an only child. Now the mother and dad are gone. Lyle is now a retired old man, believe it or not! He and I couldn't get along any better.

In England we got the month of August, only, and that was it for holidays. At Christmas, we got the day before Christmas, Christmas

Day, and the day after, Boxing Day. Then you went back to school! I remember one year New Year's Day came on a Monday, and there was school, no holiday! So by all means, put the best you've got into your life.

I wouldn't trade my life the way it's been, right through from the orphanage home till today. I wouldn't trade it with anybody for any type of life they've got. It's been an interesting experience, there's no two ways about it. I had to make my own decisions. But a lot of those things that were taught in that orphanage home have stood me in such darn good stead. I've always said you can get along without relatives, but you've got to make good friends.

I'm very thankful that in the orphanage home I learned two good things. One was to work hard. The other is to be able to get along with people. If you can master those two, you'll go through life with little or no trouble. You know, I went to England in 1977. I'd been in Canada 56 years and decided England was a lovely place to visit, but no way would I or could I live there. Canada is the best country on the face of the earth.

JOAN RICHMOND 1928-1934

It was known as Lamorbey Residential School when I was there in 1928 having lost my mother, and my father died in 1924. In 1928 I was 8 years old. I had a younger sister and an older brother. My father's parents put us there because at that time they were too old to look after three young children; they knew we would be safe.

They paid a fee when Greenwich board of guardians, later taken over by the LCC, ran it. They had some independent means. In the school I was very happy. The teachers were kind and sympathetic us children. The headmaster was, I believe, Mr Kenden, teacher was a Miss? (cannot remember) She lived in Sydenham and after leaving the school, kept in touch and paid a visit to my Grand Parents' home in Hither Green, which I always looked forward to. During the time at school, we were allowed a visit from family once a month on Saturday at 2–4pm. My Grandfather came as often as he could but my Grandmother had developed a heart condition. I was fortunate that my Grandparents had us home one week at Easter, two weeks in the summer and two weeks at Christmas.

In the school, everything was very basic. The boys played cricket and football and the girls played netball. The older girls also went to Roper Street School for cookery once a month for simple basic cooking. In the school we had four different teams: Red Doctor Arnold, Blue Sir Philip Sidney, Green Sir Christopher Wren and Yellow (cannot remember). We gained points for different projects. At the end of the each year, the team that had the highest points had a treat. It would be a trip to the owl cinema in Sidcup High Street to a suitable film for the children.

The name 'The Hollies' originated from the big house in the grounds of the home where the matron, her husband and two daughters lived. They worked in London and went to town every day. Some offices were attached to the house. A medical centre was in the home also and a dentist's room.

Bedtime was noted up to 11 years, you were in bed by 7pm and up to 14 years were in bed by 8pm both summer and winter. The housemother often stood on the stairs to listen for anyone who was talking. If she heard voices, you were on the landing for an hour. If the person did not own up, we all had to stand at the front of the bed for an hour, some of us were asleep. I'm sure the guilty person felt awful.

Very small children got out of bed before the housemother had set-tled to use the potty. I felt sorry for them, as the housemother did not have a lot of patience for the smaller children.

Thursday night was domestic night. If we had buttons off or a hole in our sock stockings, we had to mend it and the housemother would inspect it. The older girls had to mend etc. for the younger ones. During my time there, I watched the Oval [a shopping parade] being built. We received four pence pocket money a month and my sister and me would put it together to spend it as it went further.

Meals were always to time and the older children had to clear up afterwards. As regards to punishment at school, boys were caned and the girls stood in the hall. Everyone knew what she was there for. Not many girls stood there but I know a few boys that got the cane. School was as normal time 9am to 3.45pm.

When school was over, life changed from the age of 11–14. We were all allocated a job of work from peeling potatoes for 14 children and the housemother, or putting the mop over the dormitory. Two chil-dren did this, as there were two bedrooms or dormitories.

The housemother had a bedroom in between the two dormitories. At 6am, she called us to get up and she could see us through the win-dows if anyone did not get up when called. If you did not get up, you were punished. The one job every girl hated, before they went to school, was cleaning the kitchen range and lighting the fire after cleaning out the ashes. I was always glad when the week for doing this task, for me had passed. The evening job was cleaning the 14 pairs of shoes, ready for school the next day. This lasted for the week like the other jobs and then we would all change over.

We went on parade before going into school. If we passed the matron, she would walk along the row and we showed her our teeth and clean handkerchief, then we all turned and our backs were exam-ined. There were no holes allowed in your stockings and shoes had to be clean. Children were picked out if there were any faults.

On Sunday, we had a church service in the big gym. The Vicar was the Rev Goodwin who lived in Longlands Road. Being retired, he had a very stern face and never smiled or even spoke to the children. When we reached 13–14, we were confirmed at Holy Trinity and there, once a month, the housemother took us to communion at Holy Trinity.

We lived in semi-detached cottages. Each was named by a shrub or tree. I was in Hawthorn and my sister, who was 18 months younger, was in Hazel.

We had a regular monthly diet with no change in it. We played in the room we ate in, it had a table and chairs. We each had a small locker for our very precious belongings. I had a rainbow annual each year from my Grandfather and we had a doll with lots of clothes between us and comics sent by Grandfather. On our birthday, my grandfather ordered an iced birthday cake from the bakers near Sidcup station. It was delivered and everyone in my cottage shared it. My Grandfather sent us money in a letter. All our mail was opened by the housemother who took the money and bought sweets then kept them all in a tin that was handed round to all the children. I did not mind this.

In the home, boys and girls were kept strictly apart. The only time we saw our brother was in church on Sunday. The boys sat one side and the girls on the other. We were rarely allowed to speak. We could only manage a small wave of our hand to acknowledge each other. At playtime, my brother was always playing games with his friends and the quarter of hour went all too quickly.

Once a year, from Avery Hill College, students came to us, chose a child and asked us what you would like to be at a fancy dress party. We were measured and after, the students came back and fitted us. On the day, we were taken by coach, and then into the student's room, changed into costume. We then had a wonderful spread of food that we never had before. A prize was given for the best costume. After the party games, we were taken back to the home. It was the highlight of the year for us.

I think this is all I can tell you. When I look back, I feel this part of my life made me a more caring person and I had great affection for my Grandparents. On leaving the home, I took over looking after the family. My Grandparents both died at home. My Grandma at 79 and my Grandfather at 90. I did spend three years in the WAAF during the war. That was a stressful time, as I had to find people to visit my Grandfather. Eventually, our Vicar at St Swithun's and our doctor agreed that I should be released, as my Grandfather needed constant attention.

On Saturdays weather permitting we were taken by foster mother for a walk in the locality. During spring, summer and autumn the walk would be for approximately one hour each way. Tea was very simple, I don't remember having cakes. The menu for dinner was repeated over each month. I did not like fig pudding so I gave it to the girl who sat next to me or I would have got it for tea. I had letters from my grandfather, that were read first by my housemother. My grandfather always put a stamped address envelope so I could reply. The housemother read the letters and then sealed it before posting. When my father came to see my sister and I, we could walk in the grounds and sit on a seat at the cricket pitch. In the winter we had to find a seat in the gym. He did not come often but we did get home on Sundays. On returning after our time with grandparents, we sat in the train.

MARJORY PAGE and MURIEL TAYLOR 1923-1931

We both came together from a little home near Greenwich, when we got to the gate the keeper looked at his list of names and sent for the housemother from probation unit 2. When she came we said good-bye to the lady who brought us, and the gatekeeper let us in. I never saw that lady again and it was five years before I went out to the gate unaccompanied. From the day I arrived the only time I saw my little brother was on sports' days or through the fence.

I remember itchy grey flannel underclothes, white coverall, pinnafores and black lace boots with black stockings and starched bodice. I remember scalding a white enamel bucket every morning and putting it on to the front grass at 7am ready for the milk man to deliver. I rose at 6am and helped the younger children, then two girls to each dorm, would clean the dorm, ready for inspection, other jobs the girls did were preparing vegetables, scrubbing the hearth, black lead the kitchen range, clean the beds, polish floors. Even at school the girls did sewing, knitting, darning and patching but no cooking. That was learnt for college.

In the evening, recreation consisted mainly of sewing and knitting in the winter and even in summer there was no mixing between the houses except maybe at Christmas. Children would play in their own garden until the older ones put the little ones to bed at 7pm.

After the housemother inspected that they were clean, then the older girls had cocoa with the housemother before they went to bed at 8.30pm having checked and repaired all the younger ones' clothes. The only outside activities we had were girl guides or violin lessons, and the only time we went up to the shops was with a note from the housemother for collection of special rations. Once a year there was a sports day, children mixed, the band played and the headmaster watched with a cane up one sleeve. However the sports day and the swimming pool were something everyone enjoyed.

LESLIE LAWRENCE 1936-1946

One of my earliest recollections of childhood was sitting on top of a red pillar box, in a little black suit, with someone's arms around me, watching a black car drive slowly by with a coffin and flowers within. It was my mother's funeral, in Bermondsey, London. She was only 32 years old, all of which I was blissfully unaware of, as I was only five years old at the time.

Leslie Lawrence, aged three, with his mother, Florence.

The next thing I recall was being surrounded by a load of kids of similar age to myself, in a great big house, which was named The Willows. I was in a place called 'Lamorbey Children's Home', which apparently was a London County Council Orphanage. All the children – which by the way were all boys, including myself – were all dressed the same, in little cotton brown suits which smelt lovely and clean. We all seemed to be having a wonderful time, as there was a lot of laughter and jumping around, and screams of sheer pleasure as we all ran around in this great big room, which had little tables and chairs in it. Suddenly, there was a piercing whistle, and the laughter and screaming stopped instantly. You could cut the silence with a knife, all the kids just froze like statues; this was my first introduction to discipline. The silence was broken by the command 'line up', as if by magic we shuffled into two lines, 'Walk! March!' I looked over to the doorway to see where the orders were coming from, I saw a kindly looking lady who wasn't young or old, but who smiled as she gave the orders. Our crocodile lines shuffled off through a red floored hallway into a dining room, which was set out with long tables with white cloths on them, little plates in front of the chairs; which we stood behind. 'Say grace', came the order from the kindly lady, who was stood by her own table in the middle of the room, all the hands went together in mock prayer as we chanted, some were louder than others, 'for what we are about to receive . . .' etc, etc, at the end of this supplication, came the order, 'sit down'. After being seated I had my first introduction to greed. Little hands were going in all directions, grabbing sandwiches which were piled up on big plates in the centre of each table, my god if you weren't quick you ended up with nothing, it only happened to me once. The sand-wiches were always meat paste, fish paste or red jam, once a week produced the occasional sticky currant bun, which was a treat beyond our wildest dreams!

Lamorbey was a truly wondrous place: it was like living in Millionaires Row. Almost opposite The Willows, was the most imposing house I'd ever seen, or so it seemed to a boy of five, it looked like a mansion with ivy growing down the walls at the front, huge windows which were bowed, white steps leading up to a massive front door, it was twice the size of The Willows. This incredible place went by the name of 'The Hollies', and I later discovered it was the residence of the superintendent of the whole orphanage. This imposing person's name was Mr Harper. I never discovered his role in the scheme of things, except that he lived in absolute luxury.

Getting back to The Willows, we used to wake up in the morning by getting out of nice little beds, situated in a huge dormitory, we lined up in our two crocodile lines to walk downstairs in our night shirts to the red floored tiled washroom, which was a cold place, we washed and cleaned our teeth in freezing cold water, and shivered our way to pick up our clothes from the walk-in airing cupboard. We put on clean clothes every day – by the way, if you wanted the toilet, or 'the lav', as we called it, you had to go outside, through the washroom, across the courtyard, to the outside toilets. We then went back to the dining room, where after the ritual of 'for what we are about to receive . . .'etc, we attacked my favourite meal of the day. You didn't have to fight for this one, as it was bought to you on individual plates, it nearly always consisted of a sausage, tomatoes and dried egg (I personally never saw a real egg until I was put in the army when I was 15 years old.) I loved the breakfast, especially the dried egg, which apparently was imported from America. After breakfast we lined up in our two lines, and it was 'Walk! March!' to school, ours at the time of my incarceration, was called 'Burnt Oak Lane', in the town of Sidcup in Kent. We actually left the orphanage to go to school, which was just up the road from the home's back gates. We were attired in either brown or green cotton suits, so it was obvious we were 'Homesy Boys' as we were called, we called them 'the Outsiders'– ('them' being lads with parents and normal homes).

I liked school, and was an average pupil in the infant school; I was excellent at English and Cricket. We had a modest cooked dinner at school, followed by a lovely stodgy pudding and lumpy custard, yuck! Then it was back to The Willows for the bun fight at teatime, we then ran around and screamed in the playroom until it was time for bed. After repeating the washroom scenario and drinking a cup of cocoa, we then lined up for a spoonful of malt, which I absolutely adored, happy days, or was it daze! Unfortunately, the storm clouds were gathering on my horizon.

I first experienced absolute fear whilst in The Willows. One morning there was extreme excitement as we were all to attend the orphanage swimming gala, oh yes, we had our own indoor swimming pool, which was situated in the middle of the orphanage next to the school laundry. I had never visited the pool before, as the little ones didn't go there. Our two lines shuffled off to the momentous occasion, where two lines of bigger girls, all attired in blue gingham dress met us. One of the girls took me by the hand, giving me a beautiful smile; I think her name was Mary Brooks. We had never seen girls before and I wondered where they came from – boys and girls were totally segregated in the orphanage. Mary led me into the swimming baths, I couldn't believe how big the swimming pool was, she turned right with me in tow, she then stood behind me and encouraged me to climb up a vertical fixed ladder. I found it tough going, Mary stayed close behind me telling me what to do. I eventually made it to the top and just froze, as the sheer drop to the tiled floor below looked endless. I began to tremble and was about to start crying – which by the way boys never did – when Mary reached the top and grabbed my hand, she encouraged me to shuffle my way along this great big wooden shelf. Upon reaching the others I was told to sit down, this involved me sitting on the floor with my legs over the edge, Mary sat beside me holding my arm, and the most horrendous thing to me was there was no guard rail or protection of any sort, except for Mary. I remember looking down into the pool, I was trembling and I started to shake, she put her arm around me, there was a lot of splashing and cheering going on, it seemed to go on forever. The worst was yet to come. At the end of all the splashing and cheering a familiar whistle sounded, 'stay where you are until ordered to move' (I couldn't move.) When it came to our turn, Mary told me to ease back on my bottom, I then crawled on hands and knees to where the ladder was, my knees were sore, my hand had a splinter in it and the shaking took control of me again, I tell you, you could never have been so frightened as I was at that moment in time. How I got down that ladder I'll never know. Everything ached, my legs were like jelly and my arms hurt. When I reached the bottom I started to laugh, for which I received a smack on the back of my head, I was beyond caring. I took my place in the crocodile line and to my great relief I found myself outside. The blue gingham dresses were going away from me, I saw Mary look back at me and she smiled, I never saw the gingham dresses again; and I was determined to see as little of the swimming baths as possible!!

My idyllic days at The Willows were numbered, as I had now progressed to the grand age of eight. The smiling lovely lady of The Willows told me that I was moving up to a house called 'The Beeches'. I deemed this a great honour; little did I know that it was the start of my decline. From the loving, trusting little boy from The Willows, I was to become a bitter and twisted rebel without a cause.

The regime was pretty much the same in The Beeches as I was used to, but the whistles seemed much louder, orders were barked at you and it all emanated from a massive woman. This mountain of a women, always carried a child's cricket bat in her hand. I can assure you, there was none of the laughing and screaming in the playroom I was used to. You sat in the playroom on wooden forms and was introduced to darning socks, or you read comics like the *Beano*, the only trouble was the publications were ten years old. The one consolation was a radio, which was playing near my house mother. We all lined up in front of our tormentor to show her our evening's efforts at darning, if they were not met with her approval your punishment was to kneel on one of the wooden forms, bolt upright with your hands behind your head. I'll leave it to your imagination the amount of pain endured. After a full ten minutes of torture, if you cried the cricket bat went into action. 'She could have played for England! The house mother never missed. As my immunity to pain became quite high in my childhood, I decided on a different tactic to my peers. After suffering my initial spell on the bench, I got down and laughed – big mistake!! I thought my brain was going to explode, as the cricket bat cracked down on my skull. From the floor I looked up at her as the next shot hit me in the back, 'we do not tolerate dumb insolence' she thundered, apparently I had this unusual gift of registering what I thought with the expressions on my face, it was a gift I was never to lose.

I hated and feared this woman, but I was determined not to let her win. I became her favourite target and discovered that this massive tormentor wasn't very agile, that was my salvation. I never got hit on the head again, the backs of my hands got there first and some of the shots even missed altogether. I didn't mind my back being hit, I became immune and very good at dodging from side to side, and I knew exactly when to let her score.

I became a master of the bun fights for what we are about to receive was droned out with one eye open, this eye was furthest from Ma Butt's gaze. No sooner had 'sit down' been issued from her lips, I was on my chair with buttered currant bread in one hand and a rock cake in the other.

If she made the rounds – which she did very occasionally – my prizes were on my lap with the tablecloth covering them while I was munching on a diabolical meat paste sandwich, yuck! The vilest meal of all, was the weekend dinners, it consisted of lumps of green fatty meat, horrible spuds and smelly cabbage with watery gravy. Believe me, you became so crafty and sly when you were under pressure, the afore-mentioned meat went into my handkerchief and was disposed of on the first available 'lavvy' visit.

School days drifted along at Burnt Oak Lane, I liked being there because I got genuine praise for some of my efforts. I had my handwriting displayed on the school honours board; I did the poem of 'Gray's Elegy' in copperplate writing. I loved English at school and I always enjoyed History, Geography and PE. Maths was a total mystery to me, although in those days we learnt our times tables parrot fashion.

I was excellent at cricket (no, the house mother was not my coach), it transpired that I was a natural swing bowler and a fairly competent batsman. I was always picked for the first teams for the school and the orphanage.

It wasn't all doom and gloom at The Beeches, we had some laughs, but my experiences with the house mother made me think like a fox, I would do anything for my own ends.

One momentous occasion that occurred whilst I was an inmate at The Beeches, was being gathered round the playroom radio one Sunday morning to hear the news reader say, 'we have declared war on Nazi Germany from 1am this morning', we just looked blankly at one another as it went in one ear and out the other.

Air-raid shelters had been built at the back of each house and we used to practice the marches to them. You never ran, as that would appear cowardly. I hated the air-raid shelter; the stench alone was an experience you would not want to repeat. Once you were down the shelter, agility counted for nothing, as the house mother came into her own. She scored many a century down that God forsaken place!

One day came the announcement that I was to move up to a house called 'The Firs', so my last words on the majestic Ma Butt are that she was a pussycat compared to what was in store for me.

I was overjoyed to be moving up to The Firs house with the all the bigger boys. It's taken me this long to relate to you that I had two older brothers, the eldest, Harry, had already joined the army, and my other brother named Albert was still in The Firs when I took up residence.

It transpired that Albert became known as Big Lawrence, and you've guessed it, from day one I was known as Little Lawrence, I also learnt that Harry had been the toughest boy in the whole school, nobody ever beat him in a fist fight. It was natural for Albert to take over when my Harry departed.

I was exceptionally small for my age and always wondered why I never got bullied; I never had to defend myself against my peers. I always hated the thought of hurting somebody, although it was obvious I could withstand pain from reading previous chapters. The situation of not having to fight was to change rapidly. I only had about six months to bond with my brother Albert and then he suddenly left the orphanage, God knows where he ended up, although I was to find out at a later date.

At the same time of Albert's departure, it coincided with the arrival of a new house master with his new family and so began the reign of terror.

Everything happened at that time in my young life, I moved up to secondary modern school, which went by the name of 'Blackfen', this school was about a mile away from the orphanage, and we were responsible for getting to school on time as we made our own way there. It was unparalleled joy to have this freedom; of course with it being wartime we carried a black gas mask in a brown cardboard box with us everywhere. I hated practice time for putting on the damn thing, its rubbery smell used to make me feel sick. When the orphanage siren went off in the early days of the war, it was ear shattering, putting the fear of God into you. The first time I saw a German plane overhead I couldn't believe how low it flew. It was that low you could see the pilot's face; there was absolutely no resistance to these planes, as our country had no anti-aircraft guns. The only thing put up to stop the waves of German planes coming to bomb England were Barrage Balloons, which turned out to be a joke! The Germans just shot the balloons down. We were very scared, but elated at the same time, if you were lucky enough to find a piece of shrapnel it became a prized possession. When I found some, I traded it to one of the 'outsiders' for a penny, which bought me a pennyworth of stale buns from the baker's shop on the way to school; they were the cakes from the previous day. We loved them they were like ambrosia.

I wasn't very enamoured by Blackfen School and I wasn't destined to attend for very long. My childhood years were spent in the days of corporal punishment and the Blackfen Headmaster used the cane with great dexterity. Every punishment was 'six of the best' and I can confirm that a bamboo cane left you with welts across your hands or bottom. My hands were to become immune to the above punishments from the orphanage or the education establishment.

One of my greatest joys of my incarceration was visiting days. I had an Aunt Edith who came to visit me occasionally. For some reason or other I thought she was rich. She came dressed in a leopard skin fur coat, brown gloves, thick make-up and blond hair topped off by a small hat with a half veil. I thought she looked like a queen; there was nobody like my Aunt Ede. She bought me apples, oranges and my favourite of all was a slice of bread pudding, she also gave me a silver sixpence and told me to look after it. As she kissed me goodbye, she smelt so lovely and she always kept saying, 'I wanted to adopt you Leslie, but I couldn't'. I never knew what she was going on about, I was just happy she came now and then and bought me fruit and stuff. Her visits filled me full of joyous pride.

We had a housemaster at Lamorbey by the name of Mr Perks; this man was to play a momentous part in the shaping of my future life. He was the orphanage bandmaster and one day he came to The Firs house to ask for volunteers to join the school band, my hand shot up. I would have done anything to avoid the misery of The Firs for an hour or two, (anyway I liked music). The first band practice session was a complete mystery to me and all the other volunteers. I was handed a silver trombone (the only reason for this apparently was because my brother Albert was trying to learn the trombone when he was an inmate). I really liked Mr Perks, he was a patient and kindly man. He taught us the rudiments of music and I took to the trombone like the proverbial duck to water – albeit a lame duck. I had to have a little handle attached to the slide of the instrument, as my arm wasn't long enough to reach the seventh position. I loved the trombone, apparently when I blew it I had a lovely tone according to the bandmaster. The notes on the march cards were a total mystery to me, but Mr Perks encouraged me and wrote the positions for each note on the march cards, so really I learnt to play from memory and by ear. When we paraded around the orphanage, the trombones were always in the front rank, there were only two of us trombone players, and I grew in stature, to at least 4' 6", on these occasions I thought I was the Bees Knees!!!

Meanwhile, back at the ranch (The Firs to be precise). One morning I woke up to a wet bed, all hell broke loose, I was ordered to strip the bed and take the wet sheets downstairs, I was still wearing my wet night shirt I was told to go to the washroom where I was greeted by my house father, 'ah, a bed wetter eh', he shouted, 'we have a special punishment for one of those', by this time everyone was looking in my direction. I was ordered to strip off and told to go into the shower room, my house father pushed me and turned the cold shower on, I could hardly draw breath as the freezing cold water hit me. I had to soap myself all over with a slab of red carbolic soap and I noticed my hands and legs turning blue, I then had to wash myself off, get out and dry myself as best I could with a tiny hand towel, then still naked I was ordered to step in front of the house father who was stood there with a wooden hairbrush in his hand 'That looks a bit better boy, stop shivering', he barked, I was terrified. 'Hold out your hands', he bellowed, I thrust them forward under his nose, 'not there', he shouted, 'sideways, and extend your arms, you stupid boy'. I guessed what was coming next as the hairbrush came crashing down, my hand shot behind my back in a split second, the house father nearly fell over with shock of missing. His face was contorted with rage as he

128

looked at me, his teeth clenched together in a snarl; my expressive face was about to get me into more trouble. 'Hold them out properly, and keep still', he snarled, 'you two boys, hold his arms still'. Two lads moved forward and grabbed my arms. 'You're getting six on each hand for that', the house father said, and gritting his teeth he went to work with great relish. When he had completed my punishment – which I withstood without a whimper – the way he was looking at me, you could see he would have loved to prolong the agony, which he did in a way. 'Get dressed, you wretched boy', he said, 'then come back here'. I got dressed as quick as I could, more to get warm that anything else, I reported back to the man I grew to hate with a passion. 'Right', he said, 'pick up your wet bedding and put them over your head', the smell was horrendous, 'now run across to the laundry and get clean sheets and night shirt'. I felt an idiot running across the playing field to get the bedding changed. Upon my return and after making my bed, I was set some chores before breakfast. I had to clean the washroom and showers, and then polish the hallway. Then after breakfast it was off to school with the promise of some spud peeling when I returned.

After school I came back to a mountain of potatoes, I had to fill a polished dustbin full and all this was performed in the outside toilets. After I had my tea, (which by the way was without a drink for me due to the bedwetting), I was ordered to the kitchen to do my 'Cinderella' impression! I was assigned to wash up all the tea things and then polish the kitchen floor. Before bedtime the house father gathered us around him in the playroom to teach us Boxing. Yes, I was selected as the mock opponent for him to demonstrate on. Punchbag would be a better description. The first punch was a straight left, which I ducked under, 'stand still – wetbed', he shouted. Bang! In came the straight left again, this time connecting with my jaw, the gloves I was wearing were so big I could hardly lift them up. Crash! The next punch was a right cross which knocked me over the darning basket, much to the house father's delight. My nose was bleeding which he sent me to get cleaned up. After this wonderful lesson, all the others were sent to bed except for me and another boy, we were made to stand in the washroom with our night shirts on and our hands on our heads, if we were caught talking the house father laid in to us with a wooden blackout curtain pole. He didn't care where it landed, once he even broke the thing on my back. 'Right, clean your teeth now and then go to bed and woe betide you if you wet the bed tonight, he said. I grabbed my toothbrush, and I was so thirsty from not having a drink at teatime that I used to fill the toothbrush with water and suck it quietly, this way I got a drink. Needless to say, out of sheer bravado I wet the bed every night and the previous days punishments were awarded to me every time. After a while I used to stand there with my hands out of my own accord and never felt a thing, as a matter of fact I discovered that if you raised your hands slightly as he came down with the brush, it didn't sting so much.

I was to get my own back on my house father, it was ironic really, the proverbial poetic justice. He loved to coach by example, as with the boxing, and he turned out one weekend to coach us at cricket. He had the full works on, the white trousers, shirt and batting pads. He had come to demonstrate the art of batting, 'put your best bowler on', he ordered. The brand new shiny ball was tossed in my direction. 'Come along bedwetter, give me your best delivery', he called. He had never seen me bowl before, the first ball he missed altogether as it swung away from him. 'Slow it down a bit, don't be so erratic', he shouted. The next ball came swinging into him off the seam like a fast off break, it hit him clean in the chest, you could hear the thump as he dropped the bat and grunted, 'Ow!' and he fell to his knees, 'how's that?' I screamed. Funny enough, my house father's demonstrations of batting suddenly ended!

My daily punishments went on for at least six months by my tormentor. After this period in time, he'd hit me with everything he could, and I truly believe he knew I had won our confrontations, especially when I took his '12 of the best' looking him straight in the eyes and with a smile on my face.

It was then I started to run away from the orphanage, and I couldn't care less about anybody or anything in general. There were a few bright days of light relief. A gentleman by the name of Lord Nuffield had paid for the whole orphanage to go to the local cinema; I had never been to a picture house before. We all filed in to a man sat at an organ playing popular music. After a while the organ and its player disappeared below. The lights dimmed and the film started, it starred Jeannette MacDonald and Nelson Eddy, they were light operatic singers. What made the day special was, on the way out me were handed a big brown bag, which contained an apple, an orange and an assortment of sweets. What a fabulous day that was! The only toy I ever possessed was a new army search light truck that Harry sent to me one Christmas. Another Christmas I woke up to find my stocking bulging, I was so excited until I found two lumps of coal in it, nice one house father.

As a postscript, my brother Albert was killed during the war, he was shot as he landed on the beaches of France on D-Day. God rest his soul. When I got this news in the orphanage, it was the day I gave up on religion, as this has caused more suffering and anguish and bloodshed in this world. I hate it with a passion. As I said before I started running away from everything at 13 years old. After two years of absence, I was to return to Lamorbey, where I was promptly evacuated. After which, I was put into the Royal Artillery army band . . . but that's another story.

I would like to dedicate this epistle of mine to my brother Albert and to my beloved wife, Joyce Lawrence.

Bye for now.

Sincerely yours, Leslie Lawrence.

JAMES FREDERICK HULBERT 1939-1947

This account is about my early childhood memories and my later experiences of living at Lamorbey Residential School. Then I will update you and share information I discovered about myself on files kept on record at The London Metropolitan Archives.

The Hulbert family – John, Jean and James (Jim) in 1942.

I was born in North Kensington on 16 May 1932. I have only a faint memory of what my Mother looked like. She died when I was in my 5th year, 1937, which left my Father with six children: myself, four sisters, and one baby brother. Only four memories stand out from the time that we were living together in a house as a family. This record of the four events may not be in chronological order.

It was my screams that brought my Father out of the house when I saw the snake. I watched as he grasped it by the tail and beat its head on the ground killing it. The snake episode may have been the cause of my phobia and dreams, nightmares about snakes in my earlier years.

I'm unsure whether it was the same house from which we were leaving when as I was ushered through the door of the empty room: empty that is, apart from a giant teddy bear propped in a corner. I don't recall ever having played with it, but I distinctly remember screaming. I didn't want to leave it behind. It was left all alone in that otherwise empty room.

Our mother was upstairs in bed when our father organised a game for us children to play. A large bowl had been filled with water with a number of apples floating about. The object of the game was to lift apples from the bowl with our teeth. I recall that somebody, who I've always thought to have been a Doctor, came to the house, and went upstairs, presumably to see our Mother. I didn't see our mother thereafter.

The fourth memory is me pushing baby brother John along in a perambulator. After Mother died we were taken to a large house: I know not where, that must have been some kind of home, where we stayed for a while, and it was from there that I lost contact with my siblings. I now assume that my sisters, and brother, were taken into care, however, my Father took me to Monmouthshire, South Wales, where I lived and slept with a lady who, I was to find, was my Grandmother on my Father's side. On a wall there was a very large framed picture of my Father taken during the First World War. He was wearing an army uniform with a peaked flat cap and pants with puttees.

I'm not sure how long I stayed with my Grandmother in Wales, however, my Father came and took me to London, I think at about the time of the outbreak of the Second World War, 1939. I heard later, from my elder Sister, while in the care of the LCC, that he served in the Merchant Navy during that war.

I spent some time with my Father in London, in a house, or flat, that I seem to remember was the house, or flat, of my Uncle. Clearly my Father could not care for six children and quite possibly had no permanent home. One day he took me with him to a large office in a building, where there were a number of people sitting in chairs. I stood next to him in front of a desk while he talked to the official behind it. My Father became agitated: picked up a heavy glass object, that I believe must have been an inkwell, or paperweight, and hurled it at a large window, over the heads of the people sitting in the chairs, evidently awaiting their turn to be interviewed. The glass was shattered. In his temper he had, apparently, given no thought to possible injury to anybody that may have been passing outside of the building. He must have been desperate and it was possibly a cry for help. The office may have been an employment office, or more likely, he had been hoping to obtain some kind of financial benefit, or refuge for me. After he'd smashed the window we both sat on chairs until the police arrived. when we were put into a 'Black Maria', and taken to a police station where we were separated. I now realise that he must have been placed in a cell. Some time later, a policeman brought me a well filled plate of hot food. I must have been reluctant to accept it, because I remember the officer saying words to the effect: 'It's all right, your Father is getting the same'. Somebody, possibly my Father's Uncle, eventually arrived, and we returned to what I believed to be my uncle's house.

I don't recall where, or how long I stopped with my father in London, but I do vividly recall that he took me on a bus to a house that I now know to be Henniker House, in Fulham, where, upon the door being opened, a woman tried to usher me inside. I knew that my Father was trying to leave me there. I struggled and screamed to no avail. I was taken in and my Father left.

I could have been in Henniker House only a matter of weeks when I was transferred to Lamorbey Residential School in Sidcup, Kent, where, upon arrival at the same time as another boy whose name I have reason to remember, we were taken to a house named 'Beeches' and provided with clothes and our own clothes were neatly folded up. The reason that I remember the boy's name, it being 'Powderham', is because, perhaps the second or third day there, after we'd been lined up in twos in the day room ready to walk through the passage to the dining room, Powderham bumped into the wall and was taken aside. He'd gone blind, perhaps only temporarily. The last I saw of him was while he was being dressed in the day room. He wouldn't have known of course, but he was dressed into my clothes. There must have been a mix up when we'd been provided with the home's clothing, I said nothing being far too frightened. I was told that sand had been thrown into his face. I was informed later that both my Sister Jean, and young Brother John, had been transferred to the Home as well but 1 had no contact with them.

Each house on the boys' side of the Home had its own earth, and grass covered, air raid shelter. I have a vivid memory of what happened in the shelter, situated at the rear of the house. During an air raid, after we were ushered into it, and seated on the wooden forms, built in situ, either side of its length, I was caught talking to the boy next to me, and ordered, by the house mother, 'Big Miss Butt', to kneel in front of her on the concrete floor. Big Miss Butt was seated in a deck chair, as was her sister, 'Little Miss Butt', the assistant house mother. When I thought they were asleep, I curled over on to my side on the cold concrete floor.

It may have been that same air raid, while down in the shelter that we heard the whistling and loud explosions of bombs that appeared to be falling right outside, that we became trapped. Upon the all-clear air raid siren sounding, we were unable to open the door, due, we thought, to the blast from the bombs. We had to wait for it be opened from outside; possible some debris needed to be cleared.

Upon reflection I wonder why the escape ladder leading to the metal escape hatch at the end of the shelter wasn't used. Perhaps it had something to do with the size of 'Big Miss Butt' and 'Little Miss Butt', who if anything, was larger than her sister.

When we eventually emerged from the shelter, it was to find that 'Hazel', one of the girls' houses, had been flattened and we trooped over to the girls side to look at it. The girls had been down in their shelter, but it must have been very frightening for them. We were given to understand that the house mother had chosen that time to go into the house to make a cup of tea and was unfortunately killed.

I was visited twice by my Father while in Beeches when, at the first visit, he brought me an electric train set, which was set up, perhaps two or three times on the large table in the day room for us boys to watch. We were never invited to play with it and I've no idea where it was kept.

At the age of nine, I and a few other boys, were transferred further along the row of well built detached houses, to one of the big boys' houses, 'Oaks'. The younger children attended Burnt Oak Lane School situated outside of the home. The house father of Oaks at that time was Mr (doggy) Shenton, who was responsible for escorting us to and from school. One day, after a night of bombing, on the way back from school, I spotted what I was told by Mr Shenton, was a nose cone of a shell. It was embedded in the grass verge adjacent to what was called the 'cinder path' – a short cut leading from the bottom gate to the administration office known as 'The Hollies'. That of course, was before the name of the Homes had been changed to 'The Hollies'. Mr Shenton took the nose cone from me and examined it. Its nose, if I remember correctly, was a brass colour with numbers, or figures engraved on it. He took a fountain pen from his top pocket and offered it to me in exchange for the nose cone. I gratefully accepted the offer believing that I'd never be allowed to keep the nose cone. It was a fair swap. He could easily have confiscated it.

At about that time we came across masses of what looked like thin metal tape and it was explained to us, by Mr Shenton, that it had been dropped by German planes in order to foil, or confuse radar detection. We children were also told not to pick up objects such as pens as they could be explosive devices.

While in Oaks I went to band practice and learned the rudiments of music and practiced on a cornet. The bandmaster was Mr

Perks. I only recall one occasion when we went outside of the home to entertain.

Word got around that some boys were to be evacuated to the country, so my best pal, George W., and I, asked Mr Shenton whether we could go. Shortly afterwards, perhaps days, maybe a couple of weeks, we were on our way with labels attached to our collars. When I'd asked to go, I hadn't given a thought to my Sister Jean, nor young Brother John, who I'd not even seen in Lamorbey, so I was happy and surprised to see that they were part of the party to be evacuated. John was about five at that time. I was told that he'd been in the Home hospital and was suffering with mumps. He was carried in the arms of the oldest boy in the party.

My memory of the train journey to Braughing in Hertfordshire is hazy, and I don't think I had a word to say to Jean: we were strangers. At a family reunion in Yarmouth, in 1982, after the Salvation Army had investigated and got us into contact, Jean told me that the only thing she remembered about the train journey was being among a lot of nasty boys. Her husband intervened saying that it was something that she didn't want to remember: who knows? She was the only girl in the party and I put that down to the authority trying to keep us together.

Just a few of us, perhaps five, including Jean and John, were taken to a large house in Braughing where we were kitted up with clothes (I have a photo of John, Jean and myself in those clothes) and two sets of underclothes and socks. Then we were taken, individually, to houses in Braughing to live – billets. Jean came off lucky staying in the village 'boot repair shop', where she stayed after the war until getting married. The other boys, including my friend, George W., were taken to the 'White House' in Braughing; a large house, which had been taken over by 'The Norwood Homes' who now had care of us.

In 1944, aged 12, I with two other boys of the Norwood Homes, who had been billeted out, left Braughing to join Rotherhithe Nautical School, which had been evacuated from London to the small seaside town of New Quay, Cardiganshire, West Wales. The school had taken over two large houses there to house the boys. Rotherhithe Nautical School was bombed during the war.

At the end of the war in 1945, I was informed that I was to go back to Sidcup and I was very unhappy about that after the comparative freedom enjoyed while in Braughing and the Nautical School in New Quay. The other boys, they were delighted of course, as they would be returning to their real homes and families. One of the other two Homes boys that had enrolled with me, Cyril B., had left the Nautical School, because he was diagnosed as being colour-blind. I was to meet up with him again on my return to Lamorbey. The other boy, David T., must have gone back to live with his Mother in London, because I didn't come across him again.

So, I found myself back in Lamorbey Homes where I was placed in 'Firs' face to face with house father and mother, Mr Byford and his wife, and I also came to know quite well, his 'black magic', a stick bound with black electrical tape for dealing out punishment. Apparently Mrs Byford's favourite amusement was to needle prick boys' hands while she sewed replacement buttons on to clothes. Before I'd been evacuated, while in Oaks, I'd considered myself lucky not to be in Firs, because the house father, Dad Byford, had a reputation of being very strict. There were a number of Jewish and deaf and dumb children in the home at that time.

To attend the Nautical School I travelled daily, by rail to, and from, Sidcup to London Bridge with the use of season tickets, then by bus to Camberwell – 'Comber Grove' school, which was to be the temporary home of Rotherhithe Nautical School. It was later moved to Waterloo and later, as I understand it, was renamed 'London Nautical School'. Cyril B., the colour-blind boy, made the same journey to London to attend Shoreditch Technical College.

I ran away from Lamorbey twice, after being returned there, without considering the effect it would have on my tuition at the Nautical School. The first time that I did a bunk was with my best friend George, who had also been returned to Sidcup from Braughing. After being apprehended by the police, and interviewed in a cell, I told of Dad Byford and his 'black magic'. The interviewing officer seemed interested and terminated the interview. I've no idea of how long we were kept in the cell, but we were well treated. Eventually we were unlocked and faced by Mr Perks, the former bandmaster, who took us back by rail to Sidcup where we had the prospect of meeting Dad Byford, and his 'black magic'. We met Dad Byford all right, having been taken back to The Firs, but there was no punishment: 'no black magic' and I never had sight of it again.

It may be, that having not been punished for running away, I was encouraged to do it again, but with a different boy; another friend, because in the interim my best friend had been caught stealing money from somewhere in Welling and had been taken away. I found out later, that he had been sent to some kind of approved school in Grays, Essex. This other boy, whose name I still remember, and I, hopped a train to London and from there another to Exeter, without paying as we had no money. From Exeter we hitch-hiked through Cornwall and Devon passing through towns such as Oakhampton, Bodmin, Redruth and Truro, etc. Along the route we stopped at various farms asking for odd jobs for money to buy food. We also lived off the land: apples, or whatever we found . . . oh and yes, we drank plenty of milk, taken from churns, put out, for collection, by dairy farmers on wooden platforms at the roadsides adjacent to the properties. After two weeks we decided to go back to Sidcup, but not to surrender ourselves, (we had a cunning plan now to be revealed) and did the journey by exactly the same route; hitch-hiking and hopping trains.

The Homes had two main Gates, 'Top Gate' and 'Bottom Gate'. The Bottom Gate entry was at Burnt Oak Lane, and the Top Gate on Halfway Lane. Each of the gates had houses immediately inside known as Larch and Linden, as I recall; both were unoccupied at that time. We got into the house inside of the gate at Burnt Oak Lane, and slept until being awakened by the sound of boys returning from school, when we went to the window to see the boys. After they'd gone we knew it had been a mistake to show ourselves, so as a precaution we entered the house air raid shelter and slept on the forms. During the night I heard the door of the shelter open. It was pitch dark and nothing could be seen until a torch was switched on. It was Mr Shenton, the house father of Oaks. One of the boys from Oaks had sneaked on us and I felt sure that I knew who that boy was.

Mr Shenton warned us not to run away before he took us back to Firs and although I knew that we could outrun him, he being rather portly, it went through my mind, that with him being between us, we may become separated if we did run, and then there was the hefty looking stick that he carried – it looked like a walking stick. Dad Byford answered the door at Firs wearing pyjamas and dressing gown and seemed most displeased. 'I'm not taking them back', was his response. 'You've got to', replied Mr Shenton, and he left after we had entered the house. Again, we were not punished.

The Home had its own Hospital, into which children were treated and sometimes admitted, when the illnesses, or injuries, warranted it. In more serious cases children were transferred to an outside hospital. I was moved to an outside hospital on three occasions.

Once was when I was living in Oaks. We were on our way to Burnt Oak Lane school, escorted by our House Father, on the road directly outside the office of The Hollies. We'd been doing running slides on the icy road, when I tumbled and was unable to get up. The house father picked me, and carried me, as one would a baby in arms, into The Hollies, where he sat me down on a chair, then informed whoever and left to continue escorting the boys to school. Sister from the Homes' hospital arrived to examine me and an ambulance was called when, if I recall correctly, I was taken to Brook Hospital. The nurse in the ambulance was very kind and sympathetic as were all the staff at the hospital. The kindness shown to me wasn't something that I'd been used to I was most disappointed when the day came that I was returned to Lamorbey.

Once I had a two week holiday, in Queen Mary's Hospital, Sidcup, Kent. Something of an epidemic of chicken pox had broken out among the boys who were then isolated in the Home hospital. My isolation came about as a result of being sent to the hospital by Dad Byford who noticed a large sore on my stomach, after examining me, as he did each boy in turn, to see if they had washed properly, as was the practice after showering on a Friday evening. Sister put me to bed in a room with quite a number of other boys. I felt out of place, as they were covered with small spots, and I felt like an impostor. Morning came and there was I covered in small spots and the largish sore had vanished. When Sister came to do her round I was worried, because she'd warned us all not to scratch ourselves and I blurted out the excuse that I hadn't scratched myself. She made no reply as I remember. Shortly after, perhaps the same day, I was moved to an outside hospital and wondered, why me. In hospital I was diagnosed as having, not only chicken pox, but scarlet fever to boot.

At a later stage George W. and myself decided that it would be a good idea to get ourselves into hospital in order to have a holiday break from Lamorbey, and to that end we stuffed ourselves with, as many as we could stomach, small black peas collected from a tree in the home grounds from which hung pods. We thought they may be poisonous. Although we suffered as a result, nobody noticed our plight. The plan had backfired.

The toilets of the boys' houses were situated at the back of the yard where we used to play. at the rear of the house. We always had to go out to the toilets before going to bed. Never were we allowed to use the inside toilet on the first floor of the building; that was for staff use only until one night, there was a great disturbance; boys started to get out of bed to ask Dad Byford's permission to go to the toilet, and soon I had to do the same. There were up to 50 boys in the house and it appeared that all needed to go to the toilet one or more times. The outside toilets could not cope. The stench both inside the house, and in the toilets, was overwhelming. The boys just could not wait for a toilet to become available. Dad Byford relented. That was the first, and only time, that I had use of the inside toilet. Dad Byford, his wife and daughter were, not surprisingly, unaffected: they ate different food to us boys.

The home had a Tailor's Shop, that's to say a workshop where only one tailor, at that time, from outside the Home, was employed. Occasionally, I believe it must have been on Saturday mornings, Dad Byford would send a number of boys to the tailor's shop for a change of trousers, or jackets where the tailor, after licking the business end of his short indelible pencil asked: 'Wot's yer number?' and entered the boy's number on the inside of the jackets. At that time we all wore the same monotonous grey clothes. A few of the older boys in Firs, not many, suddenly started to appear wearing sports coats. I was in that age bracket, but each time that I asked Dad Byford for permission to go to the tailor to obtain one, he, perhaps not surprisingly, refused, but I was determined to have one. Two of us slipped out of the day room window one evening, and shinned up the drain pipe to the tailor's shop, and through a window where I selected a sports coat. I'm not certain whether the other boy took one, but I do recall that I hid mine somewhere in the grounds, from where I collected it, I think it was the following day, when I changed into it, and discarded the grey jacket that I'd been wearing. Strangely, Dad Byford seemed not to notice the sudden change in my attire, or if he did, he made no comment.

On Saturday afternoons we were allowed out of the home when I, with close friends, used go to the swings, etc, at 'White Bridge' playground where we sometimes met with girls from the girls' side of the

Homes. White Bridge, as its name implies, was/is a white bridge over the then Southern Electric Loop Line rail from Charing Cross to Dartford.

If we could manage to raise tuppence between us we'd bunk in to the Odeon and Regal cinemas in Sidcup, when one or other of us would buy a ticket, sit for a short while, go to the toilet area, and open the emergency exit door, when we all trooped in. I understand that some boys were caught and thrown out, but that didn't happen to me, or our small party of boys, perhaps three, or four of us.

Sometimes on the way out of the home we'd meet a certain three of the bigger girls, who were allowed out, when we'd go to the adjacent golf course, near to Burnt Oak Lane, where we had a lot of fun; boys chasing girls, and bringing them to the ground. I think the girls enjoyed it too. I don't remember ever seeing an adult during one of these times on the golf course.

It must have been during the school holidays in my time at Firs that we were taken on holiday, under canvas, to Walton-on-the-Naze. We were all very excited as we set off in buses/coaches that pulled up outside of each of the boys' houses. They were provided by the LCC. When we arrived at the campsite we found that children from Norwood Homes had also arrived. We, the Firs boys, were lined up outside of the large tents allocated to us, and Dad Byford picked out six, may have been eight, boys to each tent. Luckily I was put in the same tent as my friend Sidney H. We claimed beds next to each other, I'd started smoking while in Wales at the Nautical School, but it was a novelty to have a sly smoke in bed knowing that Byford would have to undo the rope of the tent door flaps making it unlikely that we'd be caught. One night it was very windy with the tent billowing alarmingly. Syd H. and myself let ourselves out of the tent and released two of the pegs, to which rope stays were attached, from the tent that Dad Byford shared with his wife and daughter, and then scarpered back into bed. I don't know whether this piece of mischief caused trouble for them.

After the midday meals we, Firs boys, had to line our beds up outside of the tents to rest for an hour, after which we were allowed to go into the town until the evening meal. We had a great time.

The running away, and therefore not attending the Nautical School for over two weeks put an end to my ambition to join the Merchant Navy as an apprentice. The headmaster of the Nautical School, Mr

Fuest, was a kindly chain smoking gentleman (Churchmans No. 11) who said that he had made initial enquiries and could probably get me engaged to work for Sainsbury's. There was no onus upon him to look after my welfare. I left Lamorbey at age fifteen and a half to join the band of the 5th Royal Inniskilling Dragoon Guards after passing an exam in Hither Green, a few stops up the line from Sidcup, on the 'Loop Line from Dartford'. Mr Fuest corresponded with me while I was serving in Germany.

Pocket-money day was quite an event. We would be paraded in the gymnasium, some feet from and in front of a desk until our names were called out, when we would march smartly up to the desk and be rewarded with our weekly sixpence, or in the case of older children, a shilling, after which we were expected to touch our forelocks and return to our place in line.

There was no band at the Home on my return there immediately after the war, although Mr Perks, the former bandmaster, was still there in some capacity or other. I think he had taken over as house father of 'Oaks' from Mr Shenton. It was Mr Perks who took me by rail to King's Cross Station, and put me on a train to Barnard Castle in County Durham, where I was attached to the band of the 12th Lancers (cherry pickers) until the age of 16 when I was transferred to the Regimental band that I'd joined, stationed in Germany.

The Homes in Sidcup served a very real and important role taking care of orphans, and children of disadvantaged and broken families. Looking back, I can see that the experience must have affected children in different ways in later life. For my part, although I resented the strict regime, I do have memories of happy times. Some children may have become withdrawn. I hardly had a dull period and was never short of a playmate, even if it was to get into scrapes, usually in rebellion against the discipline imposed upon us. My running away from the home was actuated more by a sense of excitement and adventure, with no consideration for those in authority who had care of us, as would be the case if one belonged to a loving family.

Having signed on in the Army for twelve and a half years with the colours, it may be no surprise that I lasted for only four, with my discharge book reading thus: 'This man is not amendable to military discipline'.

The following updates are added from microfilm print-outs taken from my London County Council files; courtesy of The London Metropolitan Archives on the 22 August 2003. Some of the material provided by the LCC came as something of a shock as the updates reveal. My thanks go to social worker, Janice O'Rorke, for kindly processing and providing the file.

The files show that our Mother was admitted to Rochford Hospital and died on the following day: the 7 of January 1937, aged 33. Copy documents also reveal that the marriage between our Father and Mother was unlawful, it being a bigamous one. Documents show that our Father is said to have been married in 1915 whilst serving with the South Wales Borderers and never resided with his first wife.

I know now, from the LMA file, that three of my sisters, Doreen, Veronica and Pam, were placed in St Hilda's Home for Waifs and Strays in Beckenham, Kent, and was surprised to see that Jean [Jeanette] was placed in Henniker House in Fulham, where I was eventually placed, however, I have no memory of any girls being there; only a dormitory full of boys. John was placed in a nursery. Both Jean and John, like myself, ended up in Lamorbey Homes. I have no memory of seeing John there until the day that we three were evacuated to Braughing in Hertfordshire.

I was amazed to see reference, in the LMA file, to my memory of being ushered into a 'Black Maria' with my Father and taken to a police station and further surprised to find that a 64 year old *Sunday Pictorial* page 3 cutting had been included in the file by some conscientious official who thought it appropriate to include it in my file. I quote the article here: 'Gaoled For Child He Loves'.

'Five days in prison separate a father from the motherless child he idolises, for whom he tramped for seven hours trying to get help. After his tramp, James Frederick Hulbert admitted at Marylebone Police Court yesterday, he smashed a window at the offices of the Unemployment Assistance Board, Paddington.'

'Hulbert who is forty-seven, told the Court he is jobless and had drawn no dole for three months. He had not even a cup of tea for his seven-year old son so he went to get help – to the police station, to the LCC and then to the Unemployment Assistance Board. There, when he was told he had to walk back to Marylebone, he smashed a window. The magistrate suggested that that was not the way to get things done. Hulbert declared: 'I am only human. What can I do? I have no work. Am I to steal for a living? I lost my temper. I am very sorry. As a matter of fact they have now put my boy in a house in Fulham. If you try to get something done for your children they won't do it, but if you get into trouble they will do something'. The Magistrate: 'I am very sorry, but I cannot pass over the smashing of Government property. Five days imprisonment'. Mrs Phillips, Hulbert's landlady in Tavistock Road, Wesbourne Park, told the *Sunday Pictorial*:

'They were a strange couple – but it was obvious how the father idolised the boy. He told me he had lost his wife and it was pathetic to see how he was really trying his utmost to see that the boy had all he wanted. It seemed as though luck was against him'.

The signed LCC Officer's reports from the file, provided by the LMA relating to our Father are interesting. 'What can be done in this case? There has never been a warrant for his arrest. So the man gets free from liability in every respect' and continues; 'There is just one thing, can the man, if he contemplates visiting Lamorbey from his present address in Wales, be refused permission to see his children who are chargeable until such time as he attends this office for a pass, when it may be possible to obtain an offer from him towards their maintenance? This appears to be the only course open, as no legal action can be taken against him.'

That to me sounds a little like blackmail, without much consideration given to our, his children's, possible wishes. For my part I longed to see my Father. The report continues – 27 January 1943: 'I telephoned the headmaster at Lamorbey about these children and was informed that Hulbert, the putative father of the children, went to Lamorbey last week and saw the two children (note – Jean and myself) without having obtained a pass. The author of the report then goes on to say how he/she posed as a friend of my Father's when visiting the basement tenant of an address in Sutherland Avenue, w9, where after the elderly tenant had searched for correspondence from my Father, she provided the officer with his new address.

The reports disclose, that as I am the child of a bigamous marriage, my father, James Hulbert, is not legally responsible for me, and that on the 14 June 1943 the London County Council assumed Parental Rights and Powers for myself, John and Jean.

'Not legally responsible' and out of work. Since receiving the file from the LMA, I've wondered how things would have turned out had not my Father been hounded? Would he have visited us on a more regular basis? Certainly he was not capable of raising six children on his own in those times of no financial relief other than perhaps in the way that he, apparently, tried very hard to do: the 'Unemployment Assistance Board' which landed him in prison.

One last footnote: the file refers to our Father's complaint that we children had been placed in separate Homes, and there again, who can say what the outcome would have been had we not been split up. Those were the days, my friends.

DAVID GEORGE HOGAN 1951-1963

It all began in 1951. I can remember a dark morning, standing on my bed looking out of the window. Down below the staff were entering the building to start their day shifts. Soon after I was being driven in a black car out through a large set of gates. I was leaving what I later learned to be the Shirley Oaks Children's Home.

When I was taken to the 'Hollies Children's Home', I was unaware at the time that my elder brother, Michael, and my sister, Veronica, were already there. My first memory of the 'Hollies' was seeing the 'Royal Coronation' china plates, cups and saucers set out in neat order on a large dresser.

My brother, Michael, and my sister Veronica, were not aware that they had any other family and neither was I. It was a strange situation to them to be told that their two brothers, Colin and David, and sister Pat were all coming to stay with them at the Hollies in Rowan House. I had not known that I had two brothers and two sisters.

Miss Long was the House Mother at Rowan assisted by Miss Eaton. They were a kindly pair and Miss Eaton took a shine to our family.

I was allowed to keep a guinea pig. It was brown and white with its fur going in different directions. There was a small garden plot, which I used to keep tidy and tried to grow things in.

Miss Eaton had a boyfriend, Eric John Sherman, who was in the Navy. For some reason I never forgot his name. He used to call in sometimes and they would take us to the local park. Whenever I saw Eric he was always wearing his naval uniform. A few years later when my family were being split up into different houses, Miss Eaton offered to take us all together in one of the smaller cottages but the authorities turned down her offer. That decision still baffles me even today.

Around 1958, my brother Michael was moved to Firs and no reason was given. Later Colin was moved to Limes and I followed him there soon after. This meant that my family was really split up. My sisters Veronica and Pat remained at Rowan until they left the Hollies.

We all managed to keep in contact with each other, whether the authorities realized that I can't say. My family was never mentioned by the respective houseparents. This was an odd situation you might say and it does beg the big question 'WHY'. Why were the authorities allowed to split up families the way they did?

One night for some reason I ran away from Rowan. It was late and I hid around the air raid shelters at the back. Some one did come looking for me but I managed to hide from them. I remember making my own way back and I slipped in unnoticed.

On Saturday mornings we used to listen to the radio in the playroom. I think the programme was 'Family Favourites', and was on at the same time each week. The houseparent used to take us to Sidcup Park where we saw 'Polly' the parrot. We would sway our bodies at him and he would copy us. There were swings, seesaws, roundabouts and other play items for us to play on. Sidcup Park was quite large and it made a pleasant afternoon out for us.

The Limes was a much larger house than Rowan. We called the houses on this road 'The Blocks'. Mr and Mrs Ernest Evans were the houseparents. We called them Mum and Dad as we had used to call Miss Long, Mum. They were a lovely couple and I have many fond memories of them.

Dad Evans collected coins from all over the world and displayed them in a picture type frame next to his private room. He also collected jitney smoking pipes and mounted them on the wall in his private room. Some of them lie had picked up from his travels abroad (I assume that he collected them during the Second World War) and a friend gave some of them to him.

One of his hobbies was making films and sometimes we would act out a western scene for him. One film I particularly remember acting out was one where we hanged a bad man – played by Kenny Last. First his hands were placed behind his back, then a rope was thrown over a branch of a tree and a noose was carefully put around his neck. The camera then filmed from the branch and panned down to his chest. The noose was removed and he then hung by his arms from the branch whilst the filming continued to pan to his now swinging feet giving the overall effect that he had been hanged as a bad man.

I found Dad Evans to be a man of many talents. He taught me to play marbles, flick cards, canasta, sevens (the card game) with eleven packs. Monopoly, draughts and chess all to a high standard as well as several other games.

Television was only on at certain times of the night. We watched programmes such as Robin Hood, Ivanhoe, The Saint, Emergency Ward 10 and Sunday Night at the London Palladium to name but a few. The older children were allowed to stay up after 8.30pm to watch the later programmes. The television was the type that fitted into a large cabinet but only had a small screen probably around eight to ten inches if I remember correctly. Television wasn't our main pastime in those days. We would play games, sports or skate or go out. We would break down old prams by taking off the top section and tying a piece of rope to each side of the front wheel to use as a bogey on wheels. We had a great fun at the Hollies. Another part of our fun was to go down to the park behind the 'Sick Bay' and jump the stream without getting a 'booty' (water in your shoes). Many an hour I played down there.

We used to play cowboys and Indians in a small wood behind the office even though we weren't allowed to play there and climbing trees became my favourite adventure. If an adult came to check in the woods to see if anyone was playing there it was easy to hide from them until the coast was clear.

There was a cupboard under the stairs where tins of food were kept. Once in a while I would sneak in and take a tin of something that I liked. Fortunately I was never caught. Sometimes the girls would raid the larder at night-time when everyone was asleep.

Dad Evans and Dad Jones (from the Oaks) spent some of their time in the evenings at the 'Black Horse' pub in Halfway Street (the pub is still there today). On Dad Evans's night off the boys would get a bit rowdy at bed time and then the whole dorm would have to go downstairs into the hallway next to the dining room and wait for Dad Evans to arrive back from the pub. We would then receive our punishment, which was usually a slipper or a hairbrush on our backside. This was the only punishment that was ever given to us by Dad Evans as far as I know.

Every Sunday morning we would be taken to church, which was around 10 to 15 minutes walk away. After the service we would go to the park, which was behind the church, and see the swans on the pond. One day at the park I met two dogs that the park keeper had. I went to stroke one of the dogs and he got excited and barked and as he did he caught my eye and I still have the scar. I was lucky not to lose the sight of my eye.

At the back of Limes was a field with two air raid shelters in it that were behind the Oaks. Every November a huge bonfire was built on the field and we used to make a hole in the bonfire and use it as a hideaway. On 5 November all the Hollies children and staff gathered around and watched the bonfire burn and fireworks were let off. The staff always had the biggest and best fireworks. There was cocoa and some food laid on for us. The bonfire would still he smouldering the next day and the farm hands would come and put it out.

Christmas was always a fantastic time for us. On Christmas morning we would wake up to find a pillowcase at the end of our beds full of presents and toys. We would spend ages playing with them before we went down for breakfast. Each house had their own dinner party as well as the party for all the Hollies children, which was held in the gym.

Every year most of the houses put on some sort of a show in the gym and our house put on a puppet show. I took part in two shows which were 'The Christmas Story' and 'Snow White'. Sometime before Christmas we were told which story would be told that year and Dad Evans made the heads out of plasticine and we made the paper mâché to go over them. The heads were then cut into half and the plasticine taken out. The heads were put together with more papier-mâché and then painted with eyes and mouths, etc. Some children made clothes for them while others made the body, legs and arms. When they were finished, a frame in the form of a 'T' would be made to which the strings could be attached. Kenny Last narrated the story.

At the big party we would he treated to a guest artist. Sometimes it would he 'Mr Pastry' (Richard Aherne) or 'Co-Co' the clown and also a magician. Each house would be well decorated with Christmas decorations and so was the gym. All the children would help to make them and put them up. The Christmas tree was placed in the large hallway of the Limes. Pupils and staff at Avery Hill College were very good to us and would invite us to a show that they put on every Christmas.

The first school I went to was the nursery at the Hollies after which I went to the Halfway Street Infant School which was across from the Homes. I was in the Limes when I changed schools again. I went to Wyborne School with Charlie Baker and Trevor Bays (who now lives in the USA). We had to go by train from Sidcup to New Eltham but sometimes we would walk to it via Avery Hill and then use the travel money we saved to buy sweets, the houseparent never knew that we did that. The train we liked to travel on was a double decker-type which made it different from normal trains and I don't think there were many of them about. It had a single compartment with stairs in the centre leading up to another seating area. We were friendly with the railway staff and they would tell us if that particular train was being used that day and we would miss our train to get on that one.

One night on our way home from New Eltham we sat and waited for two hours for the train and we found out later that there had been a massive derailment at Hither Green. We thought we would be in a lot of trouble when we got back to Limes but Dad Evans had heard the news on TV so we all sighed with relief.

Another incident that still haunts me to this day was the time when the train pulled into New Eltham Station early and didn't move out for ages. The carriages were the single type and as we got bored with waiting we changed carriages not once but lots of times and somebody reported us to the school. We were summoned to see the Headmistress in her Office and we were given the biggest telling off ever. How we escaped the cane I don't know, perhaps it was because we were from the Hollies and they would have to write a full report on the incident and couldn't be bothered to do so.

Our teacher in the 4th year was Mr James and he taught us to play football and the art of boxing. The three of us boxed for the school and became champions of Woolwich at our respective weights. We also played football for the school and on our school caps we wore the colour bands that represented the sport that we played. One of my favourite sports was swimming and the school used the pool at the Hollies. We would get a coach from school to take us to the afternoon lesson and I would be the envy of the class because when the lesson ended the rest of the class went back to school and I stayed on for extra lessons as it seemed pointless for me to go back to school only to come straight back again. I received extra lessons in speed swimming which came in very useful later on in my school life.

When I left Wyborne School I went to Crown Woods Comprehensive School where they realised that I was one of the best swimmers in the year and I represented the school in the swimming events there. I attended Coombe Hall School which was a boarding school in East Grinstead, Sussex, and also swam for the school there too. Coombe Hall only had 45 schoolboys attending and one year they entered a relay team of which I was one of the four. That year we won the relay trophy against all the local schools and was one tenth of a second outside the 'All Schools Record'.

After leaving primary school I went to Crown Woods School but my stay there only lasted just over a year. I had a fight with another boy from the third year who should not have been in our playground area. The teachers tried to intervene but I beat him up. I walked out of school that day and did not return. The rest of my schooling was taken at the Hollies own small school which was really a converted hut and stayed there until I was moved to Coombe Hall in Sussex. There was a strong sense of comradeship within the Hollies. If a child was being bullied by other children then they would receive verbal or even physical support from the Hollies children (Band of Brothers).

Dad Evans had to leave Limes because his wife died and the block had to be supervised by a married couple. It was a very sad day when he left. My memory of this period is very poor due to the fact that my time with the new houseparent did not fare so well. My brother Colin was moved out of the Hollies and I did not know where he was moved to. This had a dramatic effect on me and I became rebellious, unruly and confused. Also at this time my brother Michael and sister Veronica had left the Hollies as well (no wonder I became unstable). Due to the turn of events I was sent to Palm Cottage which was a boys-only house.

The houseparent was Mr Bean and he was a nice man but I gave him a rough time. I used to climb out of the upstairs toilet window and onto the roof, throwing tiles down at the staff as they tried to talk me down. I would like to take this opportunity to apologize to Mr Bean as it wasn't his fault that I was so badly behaved at that time. It was due to the horrendous last months I spent in Limes. That account I have buried deep down in the reaches of my mind and I don't want to relive or recount what happened, ever.

Due to my uncontrollable behaviour I was transferred to the Hollies sickbay for a few weeks for me to calm down, I assume. Later I was taken back to Palm Cottage for a while before I was sent to the boarding school in East Grinstead. I can't remember all of them, but I do remember when I went to Walton-on-the-Naze. We stayed in large marches (tents). One day I was stung by a wasp and BOY! did it hurt! I went to Exeter once where we stayed in a boarding school and I will always remember seeing the giant chalk horse that was etched into the hillside on the way. Other places we went on holiday included Cliftonville in Kent and Littlehampton on the South Coast.

When I was twelve, and in Palm Cottage, I went to Broadstairs in Kent. This is the year that changed my life somewhat. One day as I was walking along the beach I saw a black Labrador dog playing around. I befriended this friendly dog, his name was Sam. He belonged to the Coleman family and they would let me take Sam for walks during the two week holiday. The Colemans got to know me and where I was from; they were a lovely family. I was unaware at the time that the Colemans contacted the children's home to ask if they could let me stay with them and their three children during the school holidays, lucky for me they consented to this arrangement, and the Colemans became like a mum and dad to me and their children became my extended family. All my holidays were taken at Broadstairs from then on and even to this day I still call them mum and dad and look to them as my real parents. I can only thank God for letting me share their love. I would like to thank them all, especially Granny Pops, for being there when I needed them most. Thank you all from the bottom of my heart. It takes special people to accept someone else into their family and make one feel part of it. God bless you all.

My life in care was not unique to myself only. Many thousands of other children have gone through the same treadmill as I have done, and some have had worse experiences than I have. The children of my time (1950 to 1960) seemed to have had a good time. I don't recall any incidences of child abuse or sexual abuse in that time; if there were they were well hidden from us because anything major that might have happened would have been on the grapevine.

From what I have heard since from children, who were there in the late 1960s onwards things changed somewhat, but that is for someone who was there then to tell his or her own account of what went on. One must ask though have the authorities learned anything from the past? i.e. separation of brothers and sisters, keeping families together whenever possible – this should be given priority.

A question that I have asked some carers and foster parents is: do parents who have sent their children to the authorities for care and want them back at a later date get any counselling or any form of family training? From the answers that I received, only a few councils implement such actions. A child needs his/her mother's love and everything should be done to achieve that end.

A situation that I have come across is that a mother of three who had her children taken away for one reason or another – one being that she was a heavy drinker. I would ask if the authorities sent her for any professional help. I believe that Kent Social Service have a system where they do everything they can to keep the families together and give the parents training and counselling.

In conclusion to my account I would like to thank all the carers and foster parents for the hard work they do in helping families and siblings stay together and sharing their home and love with them.

I have been married to Lyn for twenty-one years now and it has been hard going at times-like most marriages, but we have worked at it and hope to remain happy for all time. We weren't blessed with children but we have many nephews and nieces whom we both love. Lyn knows of my past but we don't let it interfere with our lives. I have moved on with my life and will continue to do so.

My memories, though some are hard and regrettable, do not dictate my life, all they do is make sure that I don't follow the same road. My advice to those who have had a difficult upbringing is don't let it get you down, don't blame the past for the way you are, the life you lead is your choice. I am not saying forget the past but learn from it and move on.

I will end with The Hollies Anthem:

> There is a moldy thump down Sidcup way
> Where we get bossed about ten times a day.
> Egg and bacon we don't see
> We get sawdust in our tea
> That's why we were gradually fading away.
>
> Mummy, Daddy, I want to come home
> From this convalescent home
> I've been here a year or two
> Now I want to be with you.
>
> Goodbye all the doctors
> Goodbye all the nurses
> Goodbye all the teachers
> And jolly good luck to you.

Where shall I be tomorrow?
At the Hollies, no not true.
I'll he at home having a fag
Drinking tea with my mum and dad.

This anthem may not be the exact words that some of the children sang, as the circumstances may have altered them a little. I would like to dedicate my story to the late Mr & Mrs Ernest Evans and to my foster parents, my family and the Colemans.

STAFF ACCOUNT 1979–1980

I was 22 years old and my experience was three holiday camps with eight to eleven-year-old children as a volunteer helper and some other voluntary work with children and people with learning difficulties.

My first shift at The Hollies was working with five other staff-residential child care officers or RCCOs – to look after 18 children aged about 12 to 16 years old. They were at Reception (officially the Reception and Assessment Centre, 80 Halfway Street), to be assessed because they had done something wrong or something had gone wrong in their family that meant they couldn't stay there.

My first memory is of a younger boy being wound up by some other children at tea time. He had slightly goofy teeth and the others kept asking him if he would like some carrot juice. Eventually he cracked and threw his dinner and heavy china plate through the window behind him. Pretty spectacular since the window was closed and the dinner went straight through.

One of the older boys got into trouble for this so a sanction had to be given. The kids did not like sanctions and mostly seemed to think that it was expected of them to resist whatever it was. I think this time it was something like early bedtime, or no telly or staying in that evening. The resistance to the sanction often resulted in a physical fight between staff and the child as we tried to enforce it.

This was my first day and so I was watching and learning how to do things rather than taking part. However, I remember a team leader introducing me to my new colleagues and saying with a laugh that they would be able to 'go in' behind me. I was, it turned out, one of the bigger men on the staff. They did not know at the time that I was not very brave and scared stiff of any kind of violence.

The kids who went to Southwark on the train sometimes made it to school. Frequently, though we got a call from various schools asking where was so and so. Sometime we waited for them to come back in the afternoon and then confront them about where they had been all day. Sometimes we found out where they were because Carter Street police station would call to tell us that they had so and so with them. This meant a trio in the mini bus touring the streets of Peckham, Walworth, Heygate, Rockingham, Dog Kennel Hill, Camberwell New Road, trying to find the absconder.

One time we had a call from a school in the Dulwich area about some mostly well behaved twins of about 13 years old who were at Reception because of family problems and poor school attendance. Two staff were dispatched to visit their home, a flat near Dulwich Hospital. I climbed the stairs in a converted house to find a door immediately at the top. So when I rang the bell about halfway up the height of the door. The door opened and there were the twins. However, they were standing behind a very large, growling, drooling brown short haired dog; and because I was on the stairs its face was level with mine. Luckily, an older person, big brother we later learnt, had hold of the dog and after some negotiations he handed over the twins and we took them to school for the rest of the day.

I thought that doing the school run was a perk. It meant missing the conflict over getting the ETU (Education Training Unit) kids to go out of the door. It also meant that after dropping off I was a free agent with the vehicle for as long as I could get away with using the excuse of heavy traffic between Peckham and Sidcup. Also it was part of the job to buy rolls and doughnuts on the way back in time for the staff's coffee break at about 10.30am.

At that time kids were taken into assessment for offending. TDA (taking and driving away) was popular as well as theft and burglary. Others were at Reception for truancy. Our job was to do a court report for the kids we were key worker to. We also had to keep in touch with the field social worker who saw the family and made decisions about things like home visits and was responsible for placements. The placement was the destination decided for each kid after their assessment with us and a case conference or court appearance.

Some had a psychiatric assessment with a doctor who visited Reception every one or two weeks. The staff had a joke that doctors should have a rubber stamp with 'care order' on it because that was the only outcome he ever seemed to recommend. A care order meant that the social worker would have to find a placement. In those days foster care was the exception and so it was a choice of a long stay home with local school or a residential school like Frant Court or Burghchlere Grange. Exceptionally, because it was seen as being for very difficult kids and very expensive, there was a referral to somewhere like Peper Harrow. Sometimes we would visit a possible placement with this child. This meant a day out in the country.

The threat of physical violence was around a lot of the time. When kids were angry or upset they often lashed out. We did not call it acting out when we used physical force to restrain kids. Mostly we saw it as our job to stop them running away. The doors were not locked and we were not allowed to lock children in their rooms. This meant that if they objected not being allowed out we had to stand outside the door. This led to some spectacular fights with very strong, very angry teenage boys and girls. The technique learned by watching others was to hold down on the ground or sit on if necessary the child, until they agreed not to run or fight when let go, or until they had obviously run out of energy to do so.

This may not have been good practice or even legal. For me it was the only way of dealing with this behaviour I had ever seen and so I joined in. The us and them nature of the staff/kids relationship also meant that there was unspoken peer pressure to do as the other staff did. Later I learned that this was not the best way of dealing with things. I felt very bad about how we treated some of the kids although at the time I felt I had no alternative. I think it was one of the reasons I went for another job after about a year. A few years later I was out of residential care and working with young people to improve what they got when they left the care system. I discovered that one boy who had been in many fights at Reception and whom we all feared lived very near the office of the small charity I then worked for. I visited him a couple of times and that gave me the opportunity to apologise for the way we had treated him and to explain that I thought it was wrong.

This way of dealing with kids who did not do what we and the system wanted resulted in me getting injured. I remember a black eye I took from a boy confronted at a mealtime. I made the mistake of standing up to face him when he stood up and he just hit me. Another time a girl tried to run away and three staff chased across the field in the rain and got her back to her room. She tried to get away again and as we struggled she picked a glass bottle of nail varnish. I did not want that to get broken and injure someone badly so I concentrated on getting that off her; she bit me very hard on the arm. I had to get a tetanus jab because the skin had been broken.

There were trips away camping. These were hard work but had many benefits. First, staff could build up considerable extra time off or overtime. Second, although we had to supervise the kids we were off home territory and so could get away with more. For example, at our local swimming pool at Swanley in Kent we were notorious even though we tried to disown our kids when there was any trouble. But when on a camping trip if there was trouble with the shopkeeper or pool attendant it was the first time we could avoid getting the police or other authorities involved. Another benefit was that we had lots of fun. Camping and being on holiday was something we could all enjoy. Away from the stricter regime of Reception and in a smaller group that was usually picked to avoid major conflict.

We had a cook for most meals. They came and went from the agency pretty quickly. One introduced himself as 'Bookbinder's the name cooking the game'. After breakfast he asked me who did the washing up. I replied that there was a rota for the kids for lunch and tea but that the cook did it at breakfast. He said, 'I cook, I don't wash up', and walked out.

I hated the shift work. We did earlies, 7am to 3pm and lates, 2pm to 10pm. Late shifts were followed by a sleep in usually then an early morning that you were back at work for 25 hours. However, there were waking night staff so the two staff, one man, one woman, who were sleeping in usually got to sleep unless there was loads of noise or an emergency which was rare. One of the night staff had a habit of dishing lots of cough mixture to the kids who wanted it, evidence of cough was quite easy to produce. The shifts meant that my time off was not when my friends had their time off. So my colleagues who were also on shifts became the people I spent time with outside work.

BRIAN MAUNDER Visitor 1975-1976

It must have been in the mid 1970s that a Social Worker whose brother was connected with the residential maladjusted schools that were a great resource at the time, visited me at St. Nicholas School, West Wickham in Kent. Miss Cross was not 'by name by nature' at all. I remember her as one of the most compassionate professionals in the field. We struck up a working alliance in that she was then one of the few people in the South London area with a knowledge of psychoanalytic approaches. All my teaching staff had been hostile to such matters when I was appointed and neither they nor the education authorities could see any reason for a co-operative liaison between schools and local social services beyond the statutory requirements for financing placements. Miss Cross was, therefore, a breath of fresh air. She spoke a language I recognised from my experience as Deputy Head of the Mulberry Bush School. Before long I was persuaded to visit Shirley Oaks Children's Home in Croydon. There were already connections between the school and some house parents (Mr and Mrs Poll). But Miss Cross wanted to introduce the staff to some psychoanalytic child development theory. For some years I visited and lectured, finding willingness on the part of staff at Shirley Oaks to at least consider that early childhood, even pre-natal, experiences might influence the emerging child and adult. Some were honestly sceptical but some seriously considered such theories, altering their approach to the children as a consequence.

There came a time when Miss Cross suggested that I visit and lecture at another home in her case load. I agreed and soon rather wished I hadn't. The atmosphere of The Hollies was entirely different. For many of the staff it seemed the children were the problem. There was a strong opposition to having what was derisively termed 'an expert' coming in to tell them about child development. The willingness to consider alternative approaches to, for example, the containment of difficult behaviour seemed alien. Punishment was the main method many staff seemed to advocate and the idea that a child in care may be acting out because they were frightened was incomprehensible. Tricks were played by young temporary staff whereby they contrived to leave me with a group of acting out children about whom I knew nothing.

'You're the expert, you cope', was the clear message. When I was 'rescued' some time later there was anger that I was sitting talking and listening to the stories of the children.

'We have no time to do that even if we wanted to' was resentfully thrown at me. And it was in that that I found one of the problems that The Hollies seemed to generate. For whatever reason there was not enough usable contact time between staff and children. The causes behind this may have been managerial, financial, due to a prevailing ethos or the constant and apparently rapid turnover of young untrained staff. These were often of good intent and heart but rapidly picked up the anti-psychology attitudes of some more established staff.

My visits to The Hollies were few and I must admit I found them difficult. My concerns were raised when I found myself feeling as though I were escaping when it was time to leave. Presumably the frequent staff changes had this quality for those who stayed so briefly and left so quickly. But my concern was for the children who did not have this choice of leaving such difficult and, to me, almost ominous atmosphere.

Brian Maunder BA, M Ed, UKCP, Psychoanalytic Psychotherapist.

The following was written in 1983 by a child at The Hollies who took part in the events of that time. It was printed in the Southwark NALGO report, 'The Hollies Case for an Independent Inquiry'.

OPEN LETTER FROM A HOLLIES RESIDENT

Myrtle Cottage, The Hollies
Burnt Oak Lane, Sidcup, Kent.

I am writing on behalf of the children that were in The Hollies. I have been in The Hollies for roughly 15 years and so had most of the kids that had been moved out or may be in a couple of years, but The Hollies was their home.

When the industrial action first started, the children had meetings just like the staff, and it was decided that they would all go to Castle House, Elephant & Castle. We saw Mr Briggs (the Director of Social Services in Southwark) and he made promises to the children that they could stay in The Hollies and there was no way that they could be moved if they stayed in their houses. He even bought us McDonalds and shed tears.

We carried on with our meetings and we were quite upset when they had moved out Acacia, Elm and Firs children. We all had our doubts about them coming back even though we were told they could come back when the industrial action was over.

The children were very annoyed. Management wouldn't come to negotiate and so it made them wonder what would happen next. Then last Monday week the staff from NALGO who were asked to work in other houses were suspended, and I think that the children who were in the Hollies would have supported these NALGO members for trying to keep Acacia, Elm and Firs open. Then management had to negotiate, but while they were negotiating with NALGO, they had told the police they wanted the children moved out.

Tuesday night, Cedar had no staff so NALGO staff came in and talked to Cedar's children. Libby Graham, Officer in Charge, agreed to sleep-in for Cedar. Wednesday there was management in Pine and they were keeping an eye on Rowan and Cedar too.

Thursday night I came home from Harlesden. Marion came up to me and told me that management have said all the children who have no staff looking after them were going to be moved out of The Hollies. Some of the children had gone to the pictures. I went to Cedar where

161

the kids were telling management they had no intention of leaving.

One of the management staff offered us all McDonalds, so Mary and me went with her to get the McDonalds. We were half way through our McDonalds when she turned round and said to the children who were supposed to leave, that when they had finished their McDonalds they had to pack their belongings and get ready to leave.

We all ran upstairs in Cedar and barricaded the bedroom in Jane's room, then I said, let's go over to Rowan so we're all together, so we ran out of the house and went to Rowan.

We stayed in Rowan and barricaded the doors. The management were outside asking to come in but we refused. The children were in the sitting room and the dining room. A little while afterwards I heard one of the kids shout out, 'he's getting in the window', and then all the kids ran upstairs. I stayed downstairs by the door to make sure they couldn't get in the house. The next thing I knew, I looked around and I saw a very tall man behind me, he got my arm and bent it behind my back. I got away from him and went to run up the stairs. I looked up and there was a man coming down the stairs. Then I went to run in the dining room, but there was a man coming through there. The three of them grabbed me. One of them being [a senior manager is named here], who bent up my arms behind my back, then someone grabbed my hair, they were bending up my arms and I shouted 'you're breaking my arm' [he] had my right arm bent far up my back – every time I shouted this he pushed it up more – they dragged me to Myrtle still holding my arms. [A senior manager] was squeezing my arm so hard it was going dead, then they took me in the office with my staff Social Worker and locked me in the office. I then asked my superintendent to phone up and find out if a few of the girls from Cedar and Rowan could stay in Myrtle. He phoned up and then management said they were deciding about it. My Social Worker then went over to see one of the girls who had barricaded herself in Rowan, which was her home. So I went out to see two of my staff. I stayed there for a while then I heard from a NALGO member that he couldn't believe his eyes to what management had done to one of the girls. Some of the NALGO members and me walked over to Rowan and saw the other children.

We all stayed in Rowan, and barricaded ourselves in again. Me and my sister ran up to the main gate towards the others who were coming back from the pictures, we told them that they were trying to move the kids with force. They all got out of the van at Rowan and all the boys, except for a few stayed outside Rowan.

NALGO staff stayed around so no more assaults could be made on children. About twenty minutes later, three police vans and some police cars came down from Woolwich. They had been told there was a disturbance, but as far as they could see there was no disturbance. The children wanted to mingle with NALGO members who were very upset and angry by what had happened, but they were told by the police not to talk to the children, and more vans came. They talked to management and then some of them went over to Cedar. One of the policemen came over to us and said, Who is Karl? He then took Karl and said, 'You've got to be put in care'. Karl was put into a police van. Next was Anne from Pine, Fred was put into the police van too.

The other children ran. The children from Rowan and the children who were in Rowan at the time ran out and as far away as they could from the office where the police were. The time must have then been about 11.15pm. Some of the children went to friends' houses for the night. Seven of us hid up and got out of The Hollies. We walked on the pavement of Marlborough Park Avenue until about 1am. They said they were cold and tired and we went through Larch gate and they decided to give themselves in. Fran was taken by the police and one management staff and put into the police van. Pam, Janet, from Cedar and Jenny from Beeches walked towards the police van. Several police ran at full speed to get them even though they were walking to the police van.

Yesterday, Friday 28 October, all the children who had gone to friends' homes had been picked up. Tammy and Betty and a few others came back to The Hollies to pick up their belongings. Instead they had some shocks when they saw furniture removal vans come in to take the furniture away. Management had earlier Thursday evening promised the children that they could come back in the morning again which they were now denying. Betty and me went into Rowan to pack her clothes. When we looked around the house, first we couldn't believe our eyes. They'd smashed down doors and completely wrecked the place. We went to the upstairs of the house and looked in her bedroom. They had taken all her clothes and property and the things they thought weren't suitable to take, they threw all over the floor. They did the same with the other bedrooms too.

The office had been searched, they took all the files they could get and the rest threw all over the floor. One of the bedrooms had been left with some of the things that would have been important to the person. Two of the children from Rowan had stereos which had been dumped into the laundry basket and scratches made all over them. Half the children's property had been lost. Some of the furniture vans which had been asked to take the furniture out of the houses refused to when they heard what they were wanted for. Then because the removal vans drove back out some ambulances came. They looked like meals on wheel vans and they took the furniture instead. They never even left the animals any food. They said that the children who owned pets could take them, but those who were left would have to be taken care of by domestics or they would have to be put down. Myrtle took the cat from Laurel to save them putting it down. Some people said the kids aren't enough for them to hurt, but now they have to start on helpless animals as well.

The press at the moment seem to be taking on all the management say, and changing some of the things NALGO say as when they filmed the children on television the first time. They all said they did not want to move and they cut out the talking of the children to hide their feelings on television. I think management think we're stupid and don't understand what's going on in this dispute. In the *Daily Mail* they said that they emptied the houses in case the children came back to burn the houses down. Well, that to me is pathetic because the children want to come back to their homes so what the hell would they want to burn it down for. The press also had said that some of the children had knives, which was a lie as well. None of the children had knives on them.

Yesterday Gerry Armstrong, Assistant Director Residential and Day Care, and Paula Moore, Chairperson Social Services Committee, came to see the houses. They talked to my sister and me. They were trying to make out that the children are happy where they have been placed, but before they came Mary had phoned twice and told me she didn't like it where she is and so did a few of the others from Davey Street.

In The Hollies there are only four children left and although this is our home, it's like a shanty town here for us. We just can't believe what's happened, it was like a nightmare. I just can't sleep of a night and I think a lot of other people can't either. Why can't they see they are destroying the children emotionally with what they have done to them. They have been here in The Hollies for so long. I wonder what some of those people who come from management who helped to empty and wreck the houses would do if they were moved out of their homes and their property lost, damaged and the furniture taken away. Maybe someone will do the same to them one day and they will know how it feels. I can honestly say there is not a worst feeling than to feel lonely and hurt emotionally like they let the children feel.

Management tried to blame NALGO for leaving the children, but if action wasn't taken, sooner or later the staff would have had to go off sick. Before the industrial action the staff used to sleep in for maybe four or five nights a week.

They warned management one and a half years ago that the staffing situation wasn't good enough. Then they kept sending agency staff. They couldn't work with one staff on at a time because if there was an accident, with one of the children there would be no one to look after the other children if that child needed to go to the hospital.

So it isn't just because of the money that they had to walk out for, it was for the safety of the children which management didn't care about; and also they had lots of other good reasons to which management tried to cover up when questioned by the children.

We're not such fools as management thinks we are. When I went up to the office yesterday, which was Friday, management were eating Chinese food, drinking wine and strong drink, laughing and joking as if they didn't give a damn about the children who were still very upset with what had happened. If someone was to ask me what I thought of NALGO and management after Thursday night I would say, 'I wouldn't recommend management to even look after one child properly or elderly persons'. I would also say, 'long live NALGO child care staff'. It's also about time the press interviewed some of the children that have been removed so the public can know the real truth about the children and that they're not hooligans, like they've been made out to be.

Yours sincerely,

A CHILD FROM MYRTLE

P.S. They also turned down voluntary workers on Thursday night.

GERRY COLL 1973-1977

My mother put me in care when I was three weeks old. She kept my two older half-brothers, whom I have never met, at home with her and told her husband that I had been adopted. I was not registered as a baby; indeed it would take six years before my existence would be legalised. I was placed in voluntary care. This meant that only my mother could apply to take me out of the care system. This never happened. Still, I lived quite happily at Shirley Oaks till I was 12, when I was moved to The Hollies.

Gerry pictured in 1978.

As a youngster my favourite colour was red and I loved football. My team was Arsenal probably because 'A' is the first letter of the alphabet. Then I discovered the beauty, and frustration, of watching Crystal Palace. I swapped the very stylish and illustrious history for my local club, which I love with a passion. As the Eagles celebrate their centenary, I hope they can do so by remaining in the Premier League! For one more season at least.

From a young age I developed a vivid imagination, not only by believing that when Palace played, I was actually watching The Arsenal instead. As you can imagine this can take some doing even at the best of times. For many years my imagination would help me cope with some difficult feelings of abandonment, rejection, loneliness and increasing feelings of being unwanted as a young man. Part of my defence was that I imagined I had the best parents in the world, who they were I didn't know, perhaps a mixture of people I met and came into contact with during my childhood; it was much easier for me to do this than to believe and accept the reality. Paradoxically, I went through an experience whereby I often would tear up either something I had drawn or written and start all over

166

again, as though what I was undertaking was not quite good enough. My teachers would vouch for this! At Shirley Primary Mrs Burnham was a wonderful teacher, who taught me there was more to education than mere academic achievement. Mrs Elaine Fleming was also a great teacher, who has great patience and to this day remains a friend.

The first time I went to Sidcup was in 1970 with my foster parents Mary and Gerry Oliver and their three lovely children to visit Dee, her mother Alice and Dee's two sons Kevin and Martin. Dee is a friend of Gerry Oliver and they kept in contact long after their teenage years in South London. Little did I realise sometime in the near future I would reside a lot closer to her house than I could ever imagine. Meeting people like Gerry, Mary, Mick, Jean, June and David lit up my life. They took an interest in me and I will always be grateful for this. People like these gave me valuable respite care from growing-up in a large residential children's home.

In early 1972 I had an interview at St. Mary's Catholic School, Croydon and learned in August that I had succeeded in being offered a place there; probably on the strength of knowing the catechism. I had fairly mixed feelings as I would be the first child from Shirley to attend there and would have to make completely new friends. Wearing a cap would be the least of my problems! So I believed.

Like most children attending secondary school I was very nervous, though in a short time I became fairly popular and content with life. I was not keen for the children in my class to learn that I lived in a children's home but would say to them that I had the biggest garden in the class. By the time I invited some of my classmates to visit me in Shirley they would confirm this to the rest of the class.

In October my field residential worker visited me and said I would have to move from Shirley. This upset me but I reluctantly accepted her decision (or so I thought). Presuming I would be still going to St. Mary's I asked how I would get there from my new address. I was in shock to discover I had no choice but to leave my school because it would be too far to travel.

As far as I know my mother never visited me at The Hollies. My father would turn up unannounced and often under the influence of alcohol. I found this very upsetting and unnerving and this made it difficult to communicate or even like him. He was a difficult man and his behaviour was inappropriate towards me. Unfortunately, the bad times with him outweighed the good. He made false promises and was totally inconsistent with his visits. The last time I saw my father was 1975. The first six months at Elm were very emotionally distressing. When I expressed my unhappiness verbally I was punished for my insolence; I was also very unhappy at school. I felt the pain and humiliation of being physically beaten. Power without responsibility or accountability! Such assaults left my confidence in tatters, leaving me dispirited and demoralised. I didn't feel so upset when I was given a hiding by my housemother at Shirley because my housemother and I were together long enough for me to realise that the hand that hurt was the hand that healed. Nevertheless, I believe hitting children is wrong and it is not acceptable for an adult to enforce their own will upon a young person. Using physical or verbal abuse towards children, teaches children that you can get your own way, by these methods, which children may then go on to use themselves, for example in the form of bullying or by being abusers themselves as adults. I mention this because when I became angry before I moved to the Hollies, I used to throw tantrums and become verbally annoyed, even tempted to physically hit out at people, though I never have.

As adolescence loomed, I responded in the only way I could. I wanted to protect myself, but finding it hard to trust, I imposed a form of isolation regarding every day living at Elm.

Being of mixed race caused some identity problems – my parents would bring these to the fore by what they said to each other and how they behaved with each other in my company. It is difficult to generalise, but I think most children of similar background feel the effects of identity confusion, especially if they have not experienced living with their parents in a loving and caring environment. In my case when my parents finished their Mr and Mrs Jones scenario, they dropped and stopped their interest in me.

When I moved to Sidcup in August 1973, I attended St Stephen's Boys' R.C. School in Welling. I was extremely miserable, therefore not only did I find it hard to cope with the discipline but also we were not permitted to run in the school playground and talk at lunchtime; I couldn't grapple with single-sex education. Having lived with boys and girls all my short life until then, I was not comfortable with this new situation. I would cry a lot and being fairly tall, the other lads used to tease me about why I was crying so much. I was so traumatised by leaving Shirley and my former school, I couldn't begin to make sense and articulate this for myself, never mind to anyone else. The final straw was when my form teacher announced how pleased she was with her boys, then she looked at me and said, 'Coll, stand up, everyone has done well apart from you, let's hope for a better term next year'. I was so distressed I had actually regressed in my formal education, being emotionally entangled only made learning that more difficult. I had already decided there would be no more St. Stephens. After a while I refused to go there. I told my housemother that I couldn't face going there anymore. Under no circumstances was I returning to St. Stephen's. One morning the superintendent of the Homes came to take me to school, but I threw the dinner money on the floor and dashed out beyond the outhouse and hid behind green mound. One of the part house parents knew where I was hiding but declined to tell either the housemother or the superintendent. Looking back, it was the first time I had made a decision for myself. I was desperate and unbelievably unhappy and miserable.

I missed the children I had grown up with at Shirley, my childhood friends included Floyd, Raymond, Rodney and Clive. Last year I was reunited with Floyd who I had not seen for a quarter of a century.

One day when I was away from school, a Labour Councillor from Southwark visited our house. Councillors visited the houses to see how they operated and how the local authority's taxes were being spent in the home. Seeing me sitting in the dining room, she asked my housemother why I was not at school. After explaining the situation to the counsellor, steps were taken for me to continue my education back at my former secondary school. As was usually the case such officials rarely if ever talked directly to the children.

Thankfully, the headmaster at my old school welcomed me back. I caught the 725 Greenline bus from Sidcup to Croydon. At that time the bus went from Gravesend to Windsor. It was an appalling service and the bus was nearly always late and sometimes cancelled. Soon after commencing my daily travel to and from Croydon, I met a woman who caught the same bus and struck a friendly conversation on a regular basis, until I mentioned I happened to live at the Hollies. There after she declined to converse with me. I could only guess the reason why was because I disclosed to her the fact that I lived at the Hollies. To help ease the problem I often stayed late at the school to do my homework in order that I could spend as little time in the Hollies as possible. When I returned to St. Mary's, I really wanted to prove to myself I was capable of forming new and lasting friendships in an environment I was content in. Gaining confidence and being evermore bold I made friends with Clement, David, Lincoln, Arron and Kevin. I never disclosed I lived in care easily to anyone because I feared it would lead to more questions for which I couldn't and didn't know the full facts. However, much to my annoyance someone attending the school, from the previous children's home broke my cover.

In later years when I when commuted to St. Mary's I could see Dee's car approaching underneath the bridge in Station Road. She was with her sister June and on spotting me she stopped near the bus stop and asked if I wanted a lift? I said are you going to Croydon and she said no. She asked me if I would like to visit her and when I replied yes, gave me her address. From that time on Dee made me welcome in her home every Saturday. She showed a great interest in me and as a result my confidence increased and made living at The Hollies more bearable. She was a lovely person with no airs and graces and said, 'You take me as you find me'. With Dee what you saw is what you got! Dee's kindness helped me overcome my self-imposed isolation that threatened my adolescence, at least within the Hollies. Another person whom I got to know was Pat. She also lived in Sidcup and was the first female referee that I ever met. Two other lads and myself visited her and her family on a Sunday afternoon. We would watch the big football match in the afternoon and then play football in the local park.

The children during the four years I resided at Elm were likeable and polite and generally pleasant. Even if we didn't like each other we got by. Like me, most had no control over the circumstances as to why they were taken into care in the first instance. Most children's parents in our house would visit, some frequently, others infrequently. From what I understand, most have made a significant contribution to society in their chosen profession.

One of my happiest memories I had at the Homes was my thirteenth birthday party. I invited my whole form, plus a stunning girl, whom I had dated at Shirley. At primary school a lot of the boys went through a phase of playing kiss chase and this girl was the target of a lot of their attention. Like myself, this girl had grown up at Shirley and had moved to another home in the country. I asked my field social worker if she would try and trace her whereabouts, much to my surprise the social worker succeeded. One of the housemothers baked a lovely cake, with the words Crystal Palace and Diana Ross written on each side of square the iced blue cake. The occasion turned out to be a bitter-sweet occasion because it marked the end of our relationship. Towards the end of my stay at the Homes I briefly dated a beautiful Caribbean. We would meet at night and steal kisses, even though there was a curfew that children were required to be inside Elm at 8pm during the autumn and winter months, unless we could account for our whereabouts.

Individual houses could book the Homes' swimming pool and use of the gymnasium by booking either facility through the Hollies Office, minus the life-guards. Two staff members were required to be in attendance. Depending on demand they could only be reserved basis. During the mid 1970s there were no life-guards in attendance.

I was encouraged to go to Mass on either a Saturday evening or Sunday. The non-Catholic children could go if they wished. The choice was St. Lawrence's at Sidcup High Street or Our Lady of the Rosary, Blackfen, which was marginally nearer. We would make our way and would hop, skip and jump along the paths. In those days I wanted to sit at the back, not wishing to attract attention to myself. One morning a group of us were there without a member of staff. The Parish Priest, Father Adolph came up to us, looked up at me and asked if we were from The Hollies. I replied yes and he commented that we were welcome. I was self-conscious and felt the eyes of the congregation looking over us as though a wave of water had passed over us. I knew we were different coming from the Home. Other children were with their parents. I felt different and this made us different!

I generally formed a better relationship with the part-time assistant house parents, especially Mrs June Baker and Rita. At a time when I didn't feel listened to and had difficulty in trusting people, June was very understanding and supportive.

June and her husband Vince lived in Albany Park, with their two sons Andy and Nicolas (I think). June invited me to watch the 1975 FA Cup Final at her home. On another occasion Rita's husband Alan took a couple of the lads to watch Palace beat the Trotters 2–0. I think the reason why I tended to get on better with the assistant house parents was because I perceived they had time and more involvement with me. Even though June and Rita were part time staff they appeared to have interest in me when they were on duty. Such acts of kindness may seem small but they meant a great deal to me.

During the hot summer of 1976 I decided to write a short letter to my field social worker. I told him how unhappy and lonely I was living at Elm. As I was less than a year away from my 16th Birthday, I suggested to him that it was in everyone's interest to gain some life skills to equip me for life beyond Sidcup. My social worker declined to respond to this letter. I was unhappy growing-up in long term care for it is easy to think that not only are you out of sight but also out of mind of my social worker, who was based in Peckham. In reality, I was just as out of touch with him as he was with me residing in Sidcup.

At the age of 16 I applied for a part-time job at a newly-built supermarket close to Sidcup Railway Station, working Thursday and Friday evenings and all day Saturday. By October I successfully applied for a job as a trainee chef at Allders of Croydon. I wasn't happy travelling by the Greenline for work. I thought it was one thing doing so for school, but not for work, as I becoming increasingly tired of the journey. I hoped this would assist my case for finding accommodation somewhere in the Croydon area.

Throughout my stay most of the staff were mainly young. Sometimes this could be a bit of a problem because some staff members in their early twenties would say to me that I had no experience of life, yet I was not encouraged to grow away from a sheltered environment, therefore my wanting to learn how to cook. I don't doubt some of the staff at the Home bestowed the virtues of preparation for leaving the Hollies, but there was more theory as opposed to practice. An example was, I asked one housemother how to iron a shirt, her reaction was 'you don't know how to iron a shirt!' The simple fact was that no one ever showed me how. Sometimes it felt like the full-time staff were as much a part of the establishment as the children were encouraged to be. This was pleasing if you were happy living at the Home but presented its own unhappiness if you were not.

Such comments sapped my confidence because I was so unhappy, yet I felt I had little preparation in gaining the survival skills required to take me beyond the misery I felt living at The Hollies. When I was residing at The Hollies I couldn't lose the feeling that loneliness would not leave me alone. It kept on coming back all the time.

I didn't really want to live in Camberwell because I was perhaps too aware that my mother and her family resided there. This made me a little uneasy. I had no social connection with the area other than being born in that part of London. Rather reluctantly I agreed to move to Camberwell if it meant leaving The Hollies.

Before leaving Elm, I asked my field social worker if I could attend my review. Every six months children in care had a review and it bothered me that some of the people attending may know more about me than myself. I felt this was wrong, I resented it. Besides I thought it would provide me with the opportunity to try to express my own feelings about how I saw the present and indeed my hopes for a brighter future. I was allowed to join the gathering for the latter part of the meeting. I explained that I been unhappy for too long and wished to move on. My senior social worker instructed my social worker to tell me that I would have to stay at The Hollies until I reached 18.

When I left my housemother was crying, yet for me I was pleased to be leaving. It was in stark contrast to my departure from Shirley; which was the most dramatic and traumatic experience of my child-hood. It was so painful I had to tear up the photos of me with Pam and Doreen. Mrs Heath, my housemother, presented me with £35, one suitcase and camera as a leaving gift.

Despite having been in only two homes, I had a total of nine different social workers. You can imagine how I felt when my former housemother from my former home, Shirley Oaks, told me I had a full real brother. I thought I always wanted a brother! My former housemother said she wanted to tell me before, but felt Social Services would not let her.

I asked to meet him. First Social Services said I didn't have a brother; when I challenged, they said they thought I already knew. Finally they said he been adopted years before and they had lost the file! I said, 'I've been in care all my life. I want to find my brother. When he's 18, I want him to know of my existence, that's all. I got nowhere with them but wasn't going to give up even though one of them said to me "you're the loser, Gerry"'.

I began an odyssey through official records, which took all my spare time for four years. In St. Catherine's House in central London, where information used to be kept, I was apprehensive at first sight of racks and shelves of ledgers. But as I shuffled and reshuffled the tiny amounts of information about my brother, which I now had, I thought of a way to locate him. I knew from my housemother that my brother was called Anthony; he was five years younger than me and had been adopted in 1967. His birth certificate was easy to get hold of. I was so pleased: it was the first real proof that he existed. I used to look at it for hours.

But it couldn't tell me where he had gone. Every adoption has to be registered under a new name, not the old one. I didn't have Anthony's new name, but I did know the year of his adoption, 1967. So I went through the list of thousands of adoptees and wrote down the names of around a hundred called Tony or Anthony in the year he was adopted. I would then pay £5 to get adoption certificates with their names and old names.

Meanwhile, the Salvation Army had found Anthony through their own inquiries. Because he was under 18 they could not go to him direct, but had to speak to his adoptive mother. She did not want Anthony to see me and even my first approach left her confused, because she had been told and believed that Anthony was an only child and no one would come looking for him.

Although I could not yet contact my brother, I wanted to collect as much information as possible, so I kept on applying for adoption certificates. My persistence paid off one Saturday in July 1985. I couldn't believe it when I saw it, it was the right piece of the jigsaw, it had the adoption number which showed the location was Camberwell, in South London, and it had a date close to the one I guessed at.

Ironically, the street was the very one I had moved to when I left the Hollies. I recall asking my social worker why his attention was drawn to a building across the road from my new address, without getting a response.

I had a poor view of social workers' files. My social worker told me when I was ten years that I could look at my file when I reached 18. When I was 18 I asked if I could, and they said no. I had given them school certificates and photographs. There were variances between what the residential staff had written and what field social workers would write. I also read a paragraph that my housemother at Shirley wrote: 'Gerry is not a jealous boy, he is friendly, though he can be sad sometimes'. This was in response to a justification that a field social worker wrote claiming, at the age of eight, 'I was too institutionalised to be adopted' and another who commented, 'Gerry, must never find out he has a full brother, because he will never be able to live with himself'. Thank God I didn't believe everything that was written about me in my file, if I had, I think I may have had a nervous breakdown. Later I read that my mother had told my half brothers that 'I had died and gone to heaven'.

Finally after years of trying I was able to look at my file, even though the law now makes it possible for all children in care to see their files. I could tell lots had been removed. But some bits I came across, written when I was 10 said:

'Gerry has frequently said he would like a little brother of his own but does not know that he has a younger half-brother and a younger full brother'. . .

So it was quite clear then that things had been concealed from me. I did go back and see the file again, but it still had a lot of question marks and gaps – and, the second time around, they had even removed the page mentioning the existence of my brother! When I looked at my file I had to separate what was fact and what is someone's opinion.

I wrote the following edited letter to him:

Dear Anthony,

You do not know me and we do not even have the same surname anymore. I am open to the possibility that you may not wish to meet me, but as we are both grown up now it is only right that we should have the chance to see each other, as we are real brothers.

Perhaps I should tell you a bit about myself . . . We've had different upbringings. In the circumstances, I think I have come out of it very well, but I feel deprived of the opportunity of knowing you and growing up with you as most brothers do.

It would be really interesting to know what you are doing now and what your plans are for the future. What sport and music do you like? I do not even know the area you live in – it could be country or town or anywhere in the UK.

I've been through a lot trying to contact you and would

appreciate any form of confirmation that you have received this letter. Obviously I would like to meet you one day but even if you don't want to see me I would like just a large colour photograph of you.

Whatever you do I hope you will be happy in your life.

Best wishes

I was lucky twice. I was able to meet Anthony and get a photograph! A senior Southwark Council social worker said privately to me that they had ruined my life. I do not buy into that opinion, though they did contribute to my unhappiness . . .

You may wonder why I was so troubled by it all. I can only say, when you feel completely alone in the world with no one to call your own, having a real brother meant everything to me. Being deceived and cheated of that fact and knowledge made me feel sick deep down. It was never the fact of not being adopted myself, but the fact that I was not accorded the right of not being able to know I had a real brother in the first instance. It took a lot of bottle to go on asking for the truth and see your file: only you can judge how important it is to you. Even though it cost me some torment I'm glad I did what I did. I feel vindicated. Later, to their credit, Southwark Council gave me a fulsome written apology for my experience of their hindering me in trying to find my brother.

I had a miserable existence in The Hollies. Circumstances had a part to play in this. It is not a reflection on the children I lived with. I was very unhappy from then till I left care. Ultimately, I believe we are responsible for our own feelings and emotions.

I would like to dedicate my account to Mick and Jean Cunvin, who took an interest in me and showed me there was a world beyond Shirley Oaks. I want to pay them the highest praise.

To Mary and Gerry Oliver, who have been brilliant towards me and made me feel part of their family, giving a foundation of family life. They felt able to respond to a request made by Father Patrick Best, for people to take an interest in children like myself. Such people deserve a special reserved table in God's Kingdom for their kindness and understanding towards people like myself. I am particularly close to their daughter Sara. Like Sara, her husband Ray is very generous. Ray's background is similar to my own. A couple of years ago, he featured in a BBC documentary, 'Rough

Diamonds': a programme about adults who as children grew up in the care system. He has kindly agreed to sponsor my private book launch.

Mary and Gerry couldn't wish for a better daughter and son in law. My other good friends are Des and Rowena O'Brien, who have been very supportive over the past few years, as have her parents Peter and Yvonne. I would like to give a special mention to Megan, Bethany and Joel, Des and Rowena's children; and Natalie and Jasmine Ray and Sara's children, for allowing me to be their house sitter when their parents have requested my presence.

During the mid 1980s I was invited to join *Who Cares?* editorial board by Tory Laughland. This magazine for young people in care is now a Trust. Later I worked on the business side of the operations. Another memorable experience was meeting Diana, Princess of Wales on my 26th Birthday. We spoke for all of a minute about my work with the *Who Cares?* Magazine. When I worked with First Key, an agency that advocated the rights of children in care during the mid to late 1980s, we held a day conference at the NCH headquarters in Highbury, Islington, London. The conference was for foster carers, some of whom shared their experiences of the crushing effects of not being allowed to adopt children, whose natural parents for whatever reason refused to give their consent, even though they had little or no contact with their own children. Fostering can be a solution in meeting the needs of some children in residential care, although it is not always the answer.

My background has made me compassionate towards people, especially those who had difficult starts in life. I have been drawn to people who experienced misfortune, and those who were literally homeless. Although I have not experienced this myself, I can identify with their plight because to a point, not having had a conventional home while growing up as a young lad I have been able to sympathise with them. Given the right or should it be the wrong set of circumstances, it could happen to anyone.

Gerry recently pictured here at Anna Maria Island, Florida.

I want to pay tribute to Jad Adams, Mr Cool, whose encouragement and editorial skills has brought this book to fruition.

The reason I choose to co-write this book is because of the struggle I experienced in tracing my own background. I have been told that writing *The Hollies, A Home For Children*, it would lift some of the mystique surrounding this former children's home.

Personally, I learned to heal the scars of growing up in such places. I have forgiven my family. Over the years I have come to realise that if you can't forgive people, how can you expect in turn forgiveness for the times you let them down. God knows and gives us enough opportunities to forgive others during our lifetime. The process of compiling this book reflects my origin; it echoes my loneliness as child. At the same time it is cathartic and lays the place to rest.

I want also to dedicate my account to Misses Barbara Heath and Delia Moylan, and all the people I mention here by name. Finally, I wish to thank all the former children and their relatives for contributing this book. I hope it will be of interest to the people of Bexley and beyond.

Jad Adams'
other books include

All titles
available from bookshops
and individual publishers
and through www.amazon.co.uk

KIPLING (2005, Haus Publications)
A biography of the master storyteller.

HIDEOUS ABSINTHE: A History of the Devil in a Bottle
(2004, I.B. Tauris)
'Adams is a master of the classically lucid style enlivened by dashes of
the colloquial and by entertaining detail . . . *Hideous Absinthe* is a
model of how to convey the exhilaration of an exciting subject without
getting all melodramatic' THE SPECTATOR

PANKHURST– A BIOGRAPHY
(2003, Haus Publishing)
A biography of the suffragette leader published to coincide with the
100th anniversary of the founding of her Women's Social and Political
Union.

**MADDER MUSIC, STRONGER WINE: The life of Ernest
Dowson**
(2000, I.B. Tauris)
A biography of the tragic poet. 'Exemplary professionalism and
dedication' THE GUARDIAN

DYNASTY: The Nehru-Gandhi Story
(with Philip Whitehead, 1997, Penguin)
A composite biography of the Indian political dynasty written to
commemorate fifty years of Indian independence.

TONY BENN– A BIOGRAPHY
(1992, Macmillan)
'Told with considerable grace and style . . . candour and warmth of
narrative' SUNDAY TIMES

'Considerable narrative skill' SUNDAY TELEGRAPH

The History of

SHIRLEY OAKS
CHILDREN'S HOME

JAD ADAMS and GERRY COLL

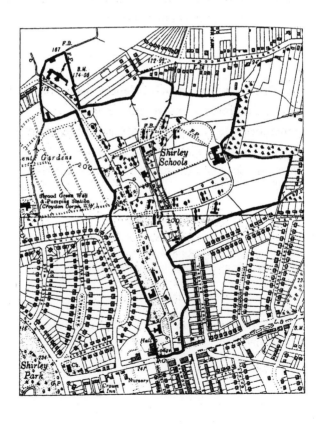

This title provides a well-illustrated account
of the history of an important children's home
at Shirley, near Croydon.
The story ranges from the Poor Law of
Edwardian England to the children's homes of
our own day. The home was opened in 1903
as the Shirley Schools by
the Board of Guardians of St Olave's Union,
whose members ran the Poor Law in
Bermondsey and Rotherhithe. Under a succession
of authorities, the home lasted until 1983.

This book gives a well-balanced history
of an institution over its whole life.
The memories of those who once lived at the home –
as far back as its earliest years –
form a major and attractive feature of the book.

Published 1999
by Deptford Forum Publishing
ISBN 1 898536 86 4

Price: £12.99
Postage and packing £2

Available at Southwark Local Studies Library,
211 Borough High Street, London SE1 1JA (020 7403 3507)
or by post from Raymond Wheeler,
88 Palace View, Shirley, Croydon CRO 8QN
email: living.history@virgin.net